To Richard, Merry Christmas 1979
Love
cousin Jac

GULPILIL'S
stories of
THE DREAMTIME

GULPILIL'S stories of THE DREAMTIME

compiled by Hugh Rule and Stuart Goodman
illustrated by Allan Hondow
photography by Stuart Goodman

Collins · Sydney · Auckland

First published 1979 by William Collins Publishers Pty Limited, Sydney

© Text photographs: Hugh Rule and Stuart Goodman 1979
© Drawings and painting: Allan Hondow 1979

Designed and produced by John Ferguson Pty Limited
133 Macquarie Street, Sydney, 2000
Designer: Allan Hondow

Printed in Hong Kong by Toppan Printing Company

This book is copyright. Apart from any fair dealing for the purposes of private study, research, criticism, or review, as permitted under the Copyright Act, no part may be reproduced by any process without written permission. Inquiries should be addressed to the publisher

National Library of Australia Cataloging
in Publication Entry

Gulpilil.
Gulpilil's stories of the dreamtime.

For children
ISBN 0 00 184 383 4

1. Aborigines, Australia — Legends — Juvenile literature.
I Goodman, Stuart, joint author. II Rule, Hugh, joint
author. III Title.

398 2 0994

contents

7	INTRODUCTION
15	THE FIRST SUNRISE
25	GURUKMUN THE FROG
35	BROLGA
47	MOOLA THE PELICAN
55	THE FIRST KANGAROOS
63	THE FIRST BARRAMUNDI FISH
73	LYREBIRD THE MIMIC
83	EMU & WILD TURKEY
90	THE RAINBOW SERPENT
95	OLD YIRBAIK-BAIK & HER DINGOES
107	WONGA PIGEON & THE WHITE WARATAH
117	THE BIRTH OF THE BUTTERFLIES

I love dancing and playing digeridoo, but most of all I like to tell people about the unique culture of the Australian Aboriginal.

The Dreamtime is very important to the Aboriginal people. It is the basis of our culture and most people don't know much about it.

Now, after my many films, I have a chance to teach you a little about my people. I hope you enjoy the stories I tell in this book and in the series of films, THE DREAMTIME, on television.

introduction

Some two thousand generations of men and women have lived and died since the first Aboriginal walked upon the soil of this land, now known as Australia. Think of your mother or father, your grandparents, then your great grandparents. Now, including you, that makes four generations, and goes back over 100 years. To go back as far as the first Aboriginal, you need to go back over 40 000 years. That's a very long time indeed!

The Aboriginal people speak in many different languages — about two hundred and thirty have been counted — and an enormous number of dialects in each of those languages. There are several reasons why there are so many different languages. Firstly, in spite of the size of Australia the number of Aboriginal people has always been few — about 300 000 Aboriginals were in Australia when the first European settlers arrived in the 1780s. This number of people would fit into one large town today, but the Aboriginal people were scattered in tribes all over the country. These tribes lived so far apart that they did not need a common language, and thus each developed a different one.

Secondly, the Aboriginal people have never used a written language. To communicate, they talked, but they never wrote letters or books. This meant there was no common written language or alphabet for all tribes like there is for the English, Greeks or Italians.

All the world's peoples have a concept of how the world was formed. The Aboriginals believe that, in the beginning, the earth was featureless, flat and grey. There were no mountain ranges, no rivers, no billabongs, no birds or animals — in fact not one living thing. Then long, long ago came the Dreamtime. The Dreamtime was a time when giant creatures rose up out of the grey plains where they had been slumbering for countless ages. These mythical Beings looked like animals or plants or insects, but they behaved just like humans. They wandered across the vast grey wastes, digging for water and searching for food and as they searched, because of their giant size, they made huge ravines and rivers in the land. Thus the world took on the shape it has today.

Aboriginal people believe that in the Dreamtime the traditional Aboriginal way of life was established by these mythical Beings; this way of life is still followed in traditional Aboriginal society today. They believe that their ancestors were taught about their tribal lands by the mythical Beings, and were told how they, as descendants of these Beings, should behave. This was their Dreamtime, and this teaching is as important to them as the Ten Commandments were to the ancient Hebrews.

The Dreamtime ended, no one knows how or why, and time and life, as we know it, began. For Aboriginal people the land has a very special meaning, for all over the land there are features which are reminders of those giant Beings of the Dreamtime. When they see a mountain or river, a rock or a tree, they think of the mythical Beings that had a part in their own creation.

The Aboriginals believe that they are directly descended from these mythical Beings. When the Dreamtime ended, the people were left with a social and cultural heritage which came from their ancestors. All the rites and ceremonies are, and always were, aimed at preserving this heritage. Their ancestors from the Dreamtime also gave them possession of tribal lands, and hence tribal land, and all forms of life contained within it, are regarded as a sacred trust.

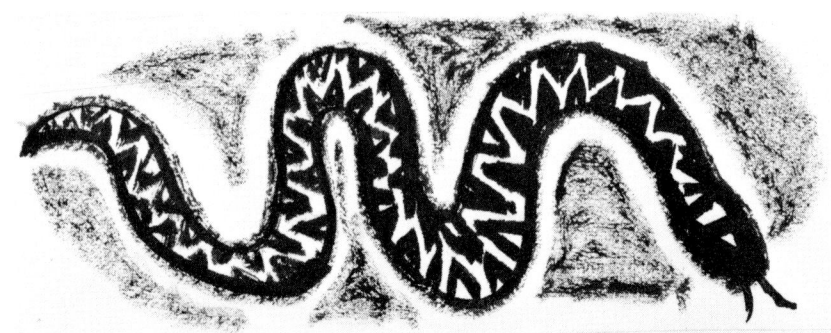

The bonds with the mythical Beings of the Dreamtime are such that they believe in a united world of body and spirit for every form of life in the land, both living and non-living. This then means that the rocks, rivers and waterholes are more than just a reminder or a symbol of the Dreamtime; they represent reality and eternal truth.

The legends in this book are some of the stories about the ancestors from the Dreamtime. The legends portray all sorts of human behaviour, including the less endearing ones such as vanity, lying, cruelty, trickery and cheating. There is a moral in these myths. As you listen to the antics of *The First Barramundi Fish,* or of *Moola the Pelican,* you are warned by the characters' downfall of what might happen to you should you fall into the same temptation.

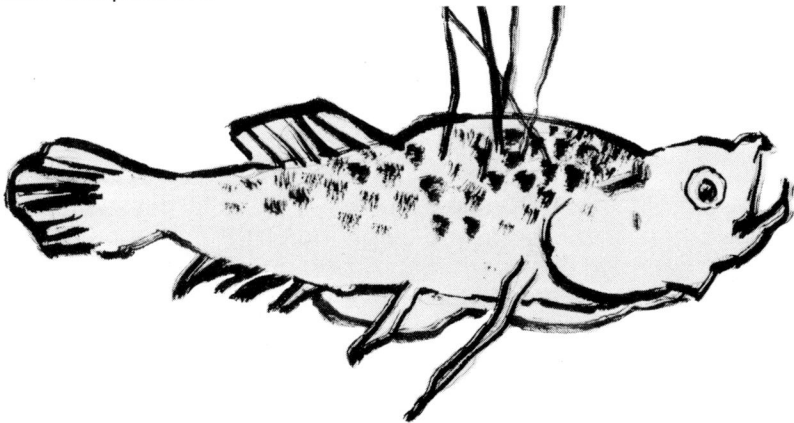

To non-Aboriginal people, Aboriginal mythology can be confusing because the characters are non-human Beings, but behave like humans. Many of the myths seem only to be concerned with a particular animal or bird. However in Aboriginal culture most of these birds and animals have a symbolic meaning of great importance. For instance, the Sun is a woman; she creates life and she is often symbolized by water, fire, earth and red ochre; the Moon is male and controls the tides and seasonal cycles — he is often symbolized by snake, dog, frog and also water.

Some people may find these legends hard to believe, but because they do not seem real to one person, this does not mean that they are not real to another. Indeed, Aboriginals may find it as difficult to believe the Bible story of Moses parting the waters of the Red Sea as Europeans may find it difficult to believe that the Wonga Pigeon's blood changed the colour of all the waratah flowers. To those who really want to believe, both these events really *did* take place.

Aboriginals believe that each tribe is descended from the Beings of the Dreamtime. Today, every Aboriginal has a special symbol — they are called totems — which represents this spiritual attachment to a particular ancestral Being. Gulpilil's tribe is the Mandalbingu tribe from northern Arnhem Land and his symbol is the Goanna. He believes that his family is descended from the supernatural Being represented by the Goanna in the Dreamtime. This belief is very important to him, and the goanna of today constantly reminds him of that spiritual ancestor.

These symbols are also important because they help to show man's unity with nature. All animals, birds, insects, reptiles, plants and other life forms, including man, are part of nature; it is only outward forms that are different.

'Cooma el ngruwar, ngruwar el cooma, illa booka mer ley urrie urrie.'

'One is all, all is one, the soul will not die.'

In tribal society, the family is very important, but the Aboriginal idea of the family is quite different from our own. The family name is taken from the mother, not the father, because it is the woman who creates life by giving birth. The family is also different because of the totems. A person in another tribe with the same totem is regarded as a brother (or sister or uncle as the case may be), even though he or she was not born of the same parents. Thus Gulpilil has many brothers, sisters, uncles, mothers and fathers! These totems help all Aboriginals to have close bonds with each other. With so many relations there's always a wonderful and deep sense of security, warmth and protection for every child. It's like having a big net of family all around you.

Most of you who read this book go to school to learn from a teacher. Not so for Aboriginal children in traditional society. They have all their lessons at home and their 'teacher' might be father, uncle, mother or aunt. Often the 'lessons' consist of watching or even taking part in the corroborees which are the tribe's entertainment. Children watch the performances of older boys and girls, and men and women, and see them make up dances and rhythms as they go along, according to their mood at the time. By taking part in these occasions, the children begin to learn some of the special but difficult dance movements which later, as adults, they will perform in ancient dances or ceremonies — so they are learning and having fun at the same time. This also means that they become very close to their 'teachers'.

The core of the Aboriginal tribal culture is music, dance, ceremonies and story-telling and all these are closely bound up with the land and nature in sacred ceremonies and rituals. These ties are strengthened by their spiritual ancestors.

To the Aboriginal, death is not the end of life. Death is the last ceremony in this present life; then the soul is reborn, thus all living people are reincarnations of the dead. The soul lives on and finds a new body to inhabit. This belief in reincarnation provides a direct link back to their ancestors of the Dreamtime.

This collection of Aboriginal legends has been compiled with the help of Gulpilil. Gulpilil learnt these stories from the elders of his tribe when he was a small boy living in Arnhem Land. The photographs were taken during the filming of the television series, *The Dreamtime.*

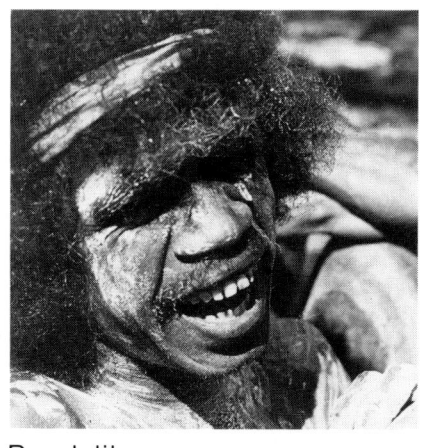
Bandalil

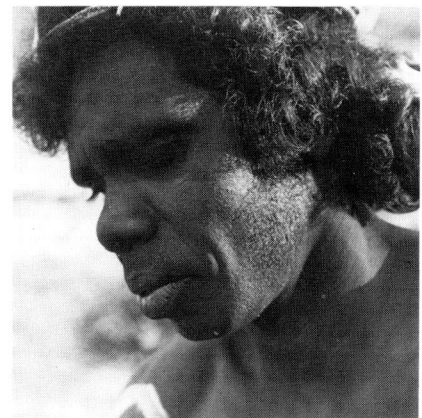
Bunnygurr

Burinyila

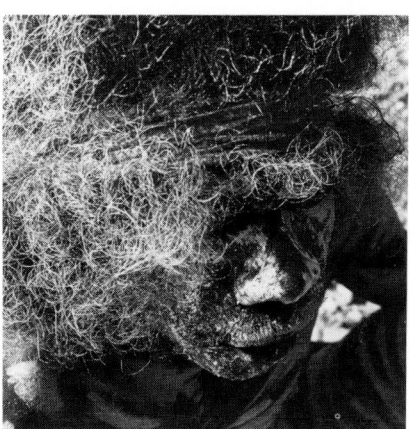
Jiborrjun

The stories contained in this book have been made into a television film series entitled THE DREAMTIME, produced by Legend Films with the following cast and crew:

Storyteller	Gulpilil
Digeridoo player	Bandalil
Songman	Bunnygurr
Dancers	Burinyila and Jiborrjun
Produced and directed by	Hugh Rule and Stuart Goodman
Photography	Tony Wilson
Sound	Brian Morris

Filmed on location in the Australian outback

THE FIRST SUNRISE

'I don't like cold weather very much, and fortunately in my lands it's always warm, and sometimes very hot! But there was a time when everywhere was cold and damp. When I watch the sunrise in the morning I remember that there was a time when there was no sunrise at all.

I'm just glad that now the sun does rise and the days are warm, so that I can listen to the birds singing happily, and the animals munching away at their food.'

THE FIRST SUNRISE

Long, long ago in the Dreamtime the earth was dark. There was no light. A huge grey blanket of clouds kept the light and the warmth out. It was very cold and very black. This great grey mass of cloud was very low. So low that the animals had to crawl around. The Emu hobbled, neck bent almost to the ground; the Kangaroo couldn't hop, and none of the birds could fly higher than several feet in the air. Only the Snakes were happy because they, of all the animals, lived close to the ground.

The animals lived by crawling around the damp dark earth, feeling for fruits and berries. Often it was so hard to find food that several days would pass between meals. The Wombat became so tired of people bumping into him that he dug himself a burrow, and learned to sleep for long periods.

Eventually, the birds decided they'd had enough. They called a meeting of all the animals. The Magpies, who were more intelligent than most of the birds, had a plan:

> *'We can't fly because the sky is too low. What we need to do, is to raise the sky. If we all gathered sticks, then we could use them to push the sky up — and then we could fly up with the sky, and make lots of room for everyone.'*

All the animals agreed it was a good idea, and they set about gathering sticks. The Magpies took a big stick each, and began to push at the sky.

> *'Look, it's going to work!*
> *The sky! It's moving!'*

The Emus and the Kangaroos, the Wombats and the Goannas sat and watched as the Magpies pushed the sky slowly upwards. They used the sticks as levers, first resting the sky on low boulders, then on small hills. As the animals watched, the Magpies, pushing and straining, reached the top of a small mountain.

> 'Munmuck, munmuck, at least we can walk about.'

It was still very dark, but at least the Emu could straighten up, and the Kangaroo was able to move in long proud hops.

The Magpies kept pushing the sky higher and higher, until they reached the highest mountain in the whole land. Then with a mighty heave, they gave the sky one last push! The sky shot up into the air, and as it rose it split open and a huge flood of warmth and light poured through on to the land below.

The animals wondered at the light and warmth, but more at the incredible brightly painted beauty of the Sun-Woman. The whole sky was awash with beautiful reds and yellows.

It was the first sunrise.

Overjoyed with the beauty, the light and the warmth, the Magpies burst into song. As their loud warbling carried across the land, the Sun-Woman rose slowly, and began her journey towards the west.

Now, each morning when the Sun-Woman wakes in her camp in the east she lights a fire to prepare the bark torch that she will carry across the sky each day. It is this fire that provides the first light of dawn. As she puts on her paint, the dust from the crushed red ochre colours the early morning clouds a beautiful soft red.

Then she takes up her torch, and begins her daily journey across the sky.

When she reaches the western edge of the world, she extinguishes her flaming bark torch. Then she sits down, and repaints herself in brilliant reds and yellows, ready for her journey through a long underground passage, back to her camp in the east.

So that is why, to this day, every morning when the Sun-Woman wakes and lights her early morning fire, all the magpies greet her with their beautiful song.

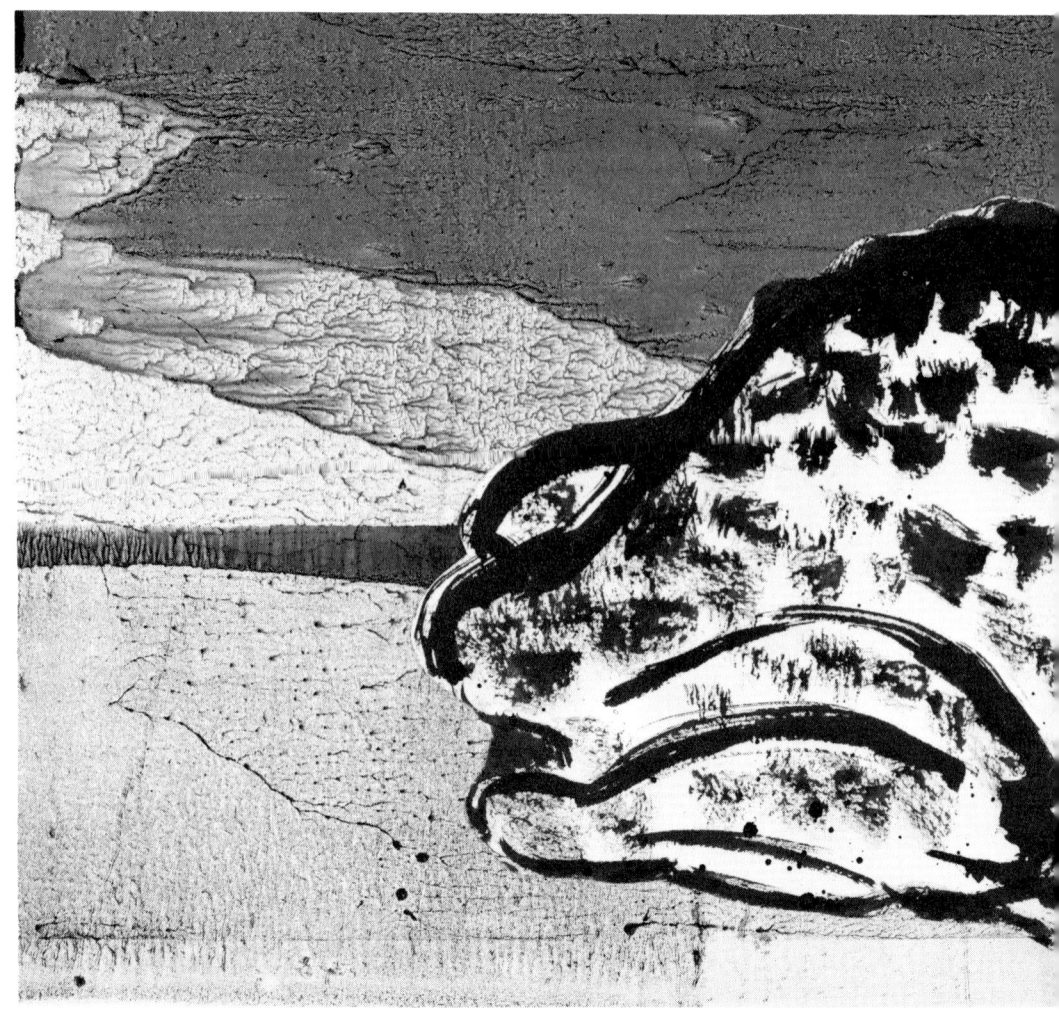

GURUKMUN THE FROG

'Frogs really like water, and whenever it rains you can hear them as they croak with delight. There's a legend we have about a frog who liked water so much that he drank all the water he could find. As he was a giant sized frog, and was very, very greedy, he drank all the water in the whole land! That didn't leave a drop for anybody else who was thirsty!

   Here's how all the birds and animals managed to get the water back from the greedy frog.'

GURUKMUN THE FROG

A long time ago, way back in the Dreamtime, there lived a big, big frog, called Gurukmun. He was easily the biggest frog in the whole land, so big that, as he hopped, each hop would make the earth shake. Gurukmun didn't live in a river or creek because there were none big enough, and besides, he liked to hop about on dry land.

One very hot day, all the animals were gathered at a waterhole. They were sitting around, chatting about the hot day while the little ones were playing in the water. Then they heard Gurukmun's boolumph! boolumph! boolumph! as he hopped towards the waterhole.

The animals watched as he plopped down beside the waterhole, and started to drink. And he drank, and he drank, and he drank, until all the water was gone! Where the beautiful waterhole had been, there was nothing but a big muddy patch!

Then Gurukmun hopped away to look for another waterhole.

One waterhole was not enough for a huge Frog like Gurukmun. And what's more, he was feeling particularly thirsty. He hopped until he came to a river, and he began to drink. Soon, all the water in the river was gone!

Gurukmun rubbed his big green belly. He was still very thirsty, so he hopped down to the ocean, and began to drink.

He drank, and he drank, and he drank, slurping up the ocean, and as he drank, his belly grew bigger and bigger and bigger. When all the water in the ocean was gone, Gurukmun was still thirsty!

The animals began to worry. Gurukmun was drinking all their water — soon there would be none left. They watched as Gurukmun went from river to lake to waterhole, drinking each one dry. And he didn't stop until all the water in the whole world was gone. All inside his enormous green belly!

Then Gurukmun, with all the water in the whole land inside him, hopped slowly up on to the top of an enormous mountain. And there he sat, looking out over the dry brown land.

The other animals became very worried. Now they had nothing to drink, and there was no water for the trees and the grass — Gurukmun had taken it all. What were they to do?

The Emu and the Goanna went to see the wise old Wombat.

'Wombat, there is no water. Gurukmun has it all, and if we don't get it back, then we will all die!'

The Wombat called a meeting. All the animals gathered at the bottom of Gurukmun's mountain. The Kookaburra flew up to Gurukmun to ask if he would give some of the water back.

'Kokarah, kook kook kook! Gurukmun, you don't need all that water. Don't be greedy, why don't you share the water with all of us?'

But Gurukmun just sat there, big and fat and green. He had all the water, and he wasn't going to part with any of it.

How were they going to get the water back? The Possum suggested frightening him. If Gurukmun had a fright, then he might cough some of the water out. But how do you frighten the biggest Frog in all the world? The Goanna thought that if someone could tickle Gurukmun's nose, then he might sneeze some of the water out. But how were they to reach his nose? It was such a long way up, and anyway, he probably wasn't ticklish.

Then the wise old Wombat had an idea. What if we make him laugh? If Gurukmun laughed, then surely all the water would come gushing out. The animals thought about it. It was the best idea, and if they didn't soon do something, they would all shrivel up and die. So it was decided. They would make him laugh.

The Kookaburra was the first to try. He would tell Gurukmun his funniest jokes — he would surely laugh at those, they always made Kookaburras laugh. He flew up to Gurukmun.

'Did you hear the one about kook, kooka, kook-u-ah-kook-kook.?'

The Kookaburra flapped about, laughing his head off. But Gurukmun didn't laugh. He just sat there, with all the water in his big fat belly.

The Emu thought he would try.

'I'll do my funniest walk. That's sure to make him laugh.'

The Emu strutted up to the Frog. He began strutting around, his long neck snaking back and forth, his brown eyes rolling. The other animals thought it was very funny, they had tears running down their faces. Even the Emu started to laugh.

But Gurukmun didn't laugh. He just sat there. Then the Kangaroo had an idea.

'Funny hops, that's the answer! I do the best funny hops in the whole land!'

So he hopped up to the Frog.

'Ready frog? Here we go! The funniest hops you've ever seen!'

And the Kangaroo began to hop about. Sideways hops, little hops, big hops, even backward hops. Just as he was about to do his biggest hop, his foot went down a hole, and the Kangaroo fell flat on his face! The other animals roared with laughter. The Kangaroo looked so silly, lying there, flat on his face in the dust. But the Frog didn't laugh.

The animals didn't know what to do. Perhaps Frogs didn't laugh.

'Yes they do. I've seen them. Everytime it rains. And I ought to know!'

It was old Nabunum, the Eel. He wriggled up to the front of the meeting. The Magpies started to giggle. He looked so funny, out on dry land. Nabunum glared at them.

> 'What do you think is so funny? If someone took away the trees, you wouldn't think it was funny! I'll show you how to make this Frog laugh. And he'll laugh so much, that all the water will come out!'

So Nabunum wriggled up to Gurukmun. And he began to dance. He did look silly, an old Eel, wriggling about, trying to dance like the Brolga.

Gurukmun looked down at the old Eel. Nabunum was writhing and thrashing, wriggling and crawling, curling and uncurling, twisting in and out and all around himself. Then suddenly he stopped! He was stuck!

The animals burst out laughing. The Wombat rolled about in the dust. Old Nabunum, all tied up. It was the funniest thing he had ever seen!

Then the animals heard it. A huge gurgling noise. They looked up, and it was Gurukmun. An enormous grin stretched across his big green face. Nabunum struggled to untie himself, and as he struggled, Gurukmun began to laugh in earnest. Great big laughs. And as he laughed, the water started to come from out of his enormous mouth.

> 'I was right, I was right! Here comes our water!'

And Gurukmun laughed so much, that all the water flowed back to fill the oceans and lakes, the rivers and billabongs, the lagoons and the waterholes.

The animals rushed up to old Nabunum, and helped him to untie himself.

> 'Thank you Nabunum, your funny dance has saved us all!'

And Gurukmun, the greedy Frog, hopped away and has never been seen again. But even to this day the Aboriginals have a special regard for frogs because they know the story of Gurukmun in the Dreamtime.

BROLGA

'Ah beautiful brolgas! I can sit and watch them for hours, as they go through their lovely dances. Brolgas look a bit like emus because they have long legs and big bodies. But they are much prettier, with their pink and grey colouring.

Sometimes, I try to imitate their wonderful movements, but it's very hard to do them well.'

BROLGA

Long ago, back in the Dreamtime, there was a very beautiful young girl, named Brolga. Even though she was very young, Brolga was the best dancer in the whole land. Everyone in the tribe was very proud of Brolga, her dancing was so graceful, and her movements so special. When she danced, the old people would sit around and say,

> 'She dances so well. It makes us proud that she's part of our tribe.'

> 'Look at Brolga, she must be the best dancer in the whole land!'

Now Brolga hadn't always been such a good dancer. When she was a very little girl, she used to get up very early in the morning, and creep past her sleeping brothers and sisters, out of the gunyah and to the plains around her camp. Once there, she would practise swooshing her arms like the Pelican, parading like the Emu, and whirling like the wind. Brolga soon became so good that the rest of the tribe asked her to join in their dances.

But Brolga didn't just do the old dances. She liked to make up new ones. Dances about the trees and the wind, dances about the Spirits and the animals. The dances that Brolga invented were so good, that people from other tribes would come just to see her dance. The more she danced, the more famous she became.

The old men of the tribe were very proud of her. Never had there ever been anyone as talented as Brolga. And they were sure that her dancing would make their tribe the most famous in the whole land. They would sit and watch as the beautiful young girl whirled and twirled — she seemed to fly through her dances.

Sometimes the old people would worry. Brolga was very pretty and very famous. What if she became too proud? They worried that she would become vain, and ask for special treatment. But she never did. Each day found her the same happy modest Brolga as the day before.

Each day, Brolga would spend some time gathering food with the women and at night she would dance for the rest of the tribe.

One day, Brolga went off by herself to dance. She went out onto the dry red plain near her camp. On this plain, was her favourite tree, a big old coolibah tree. Brolga began to dance in its shade, moving with the shadow of the old tree's branches. As the wind swayed the tree, Brolga swayed, dancing out into the sunlight. The early morning sun fell on her face and with her arms floating out she spun for the sheer joy of it.

As the little puffs of dust rose from her feet, an evil Spirit, Waiwera, looked down from his home in the Milky Way, and saw Brolga. She was without doubt the most graceful and beautiful girl he had ever seen. Waiwera decided that Brolga must be his. He would steal her to be his woman!

Waiwera quickly spun himself into a whirlwind, a willy-willy, and flew down onto the plain. Brolga saw the willy-willy swirling across the plain. It looked so very pretty, a gentle column of dust spiralling upwards.

Brolga didn't know that it was the evil Spirit, Waiwera!

As the wind came closer to Brolga, it made a sudden great roaring sound, and enclosed her. Brolga was swept off her feet. She was caught! The wind roared, and Brolga thrashed, but it was no use, she could not escape! Far away she could see the big old coolibah tree, and near it the camp of her tribe. She began to cry.

When Brolga's tribe discovered she was missing, they went looking for her.

'Maybe another tribe has stolen her.'

'No, we would have heard her cries.'

'If we can find her tracks, then we will be able to follow them. They will show us where she has gone.'

But the wind had covered her tracks. The tribe searched everywhere for her. They found the big old coolibah tree.

'She used to come here to dance, but there are no tracks.'

Then they saw the path where the willy-willy had been. One of the old men suggested they follow the path of the willy-willy, perhaps that would take them to Brolga. So the tribe set out.

For several days, they followed the path of the willy-willy, until they came to a hill overlooking a small plain. There below them, they saw the evil Spirit, Waiwera, and with him was his captive, Brolga!

The whole tribe rushed down hurling their spears and their boomerangs. Waiwera, seeing them coming, began to spin the whirlwind faster. Brolga was now his, and the evil, jealous Spirit, realizing that he couldn't escape with her, decided that no one would have her. The whirlwind swirled around Brolga, and just as the tribe reached her, she vanished!

Brolga's tribe watched as the willy-willy wound its way slowly up into the sky. On the spot where it had been, there now stood a big old coolibah tree. But there was no sign of Brolga.

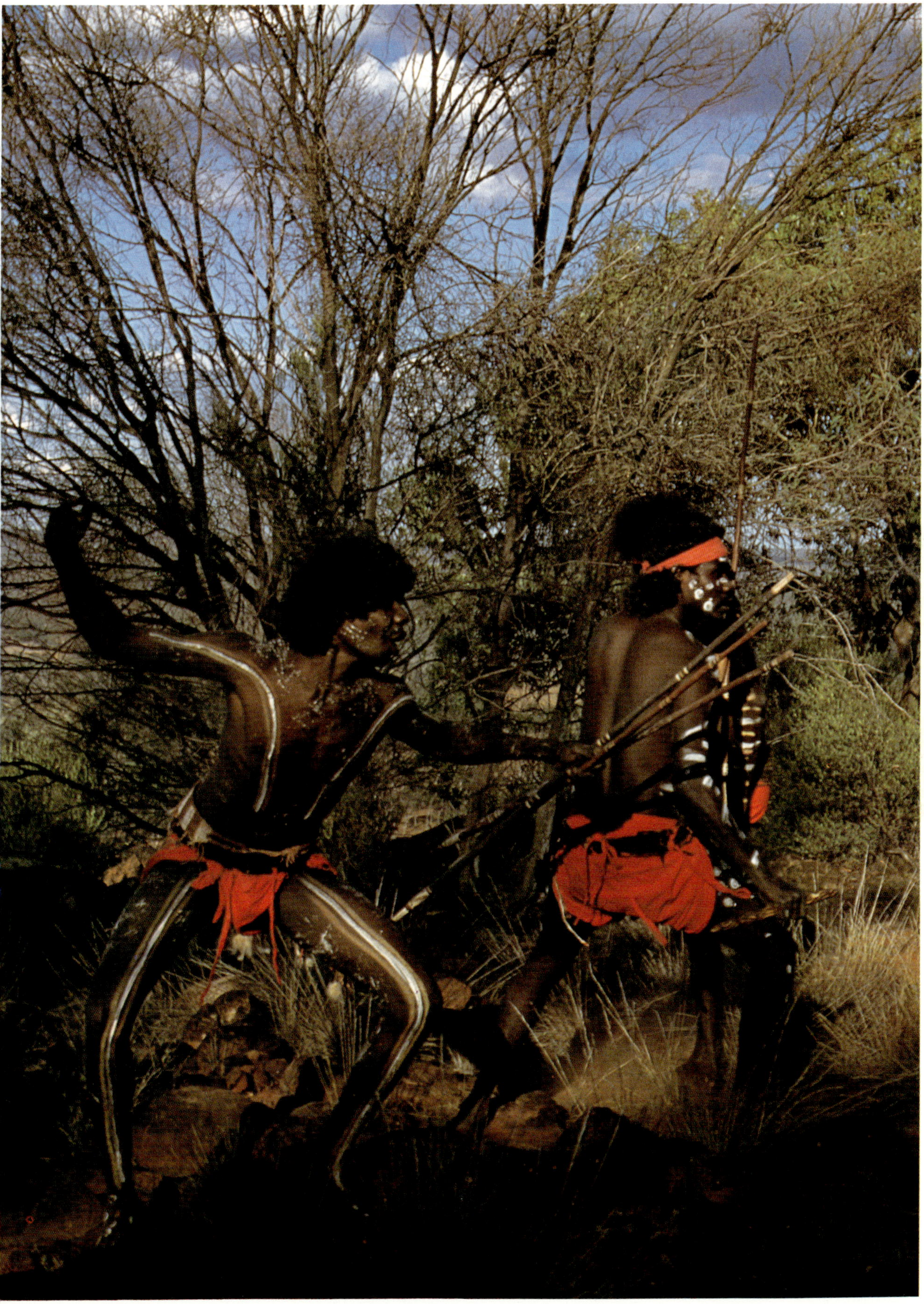

They knew that the evil Spirit, Waiwera, had returned to his home in the two black holes in the Milky Way. The old people shuddered and hoped that they would never have to pass along the Milky Way, for to do so, they would have to pass the two black holes where Waiwera lived.

As they stood near the tree which Waiwera had left, one of the children shouted,

> 'Look! Look! There is a bird! A bird we have never seen before!'

As they watched, a beautiful tall grey bird appeared from behind the tree. Not even the old people had seen one like it. The bird slowly stretched its wings, and instead of flying away, it began to dance, making the same graceful moves that Brolga used to make.

The bird danced, taking long, hopping steps, and floating on its graceful wings.

The men called out,

>*'It's Brolga! It's Brolga!*
>*See, the bird is dancing just like Brolga!'*

And the bird seemed to understand. It pranced slowly towards them, and with one last graceful bound, flew up into the air, and away!

Then they all knew that the wicked Waiwera had changed Brolga into a bird. A bird which the Aboriginals, from that day onwards, have always called the brolga.

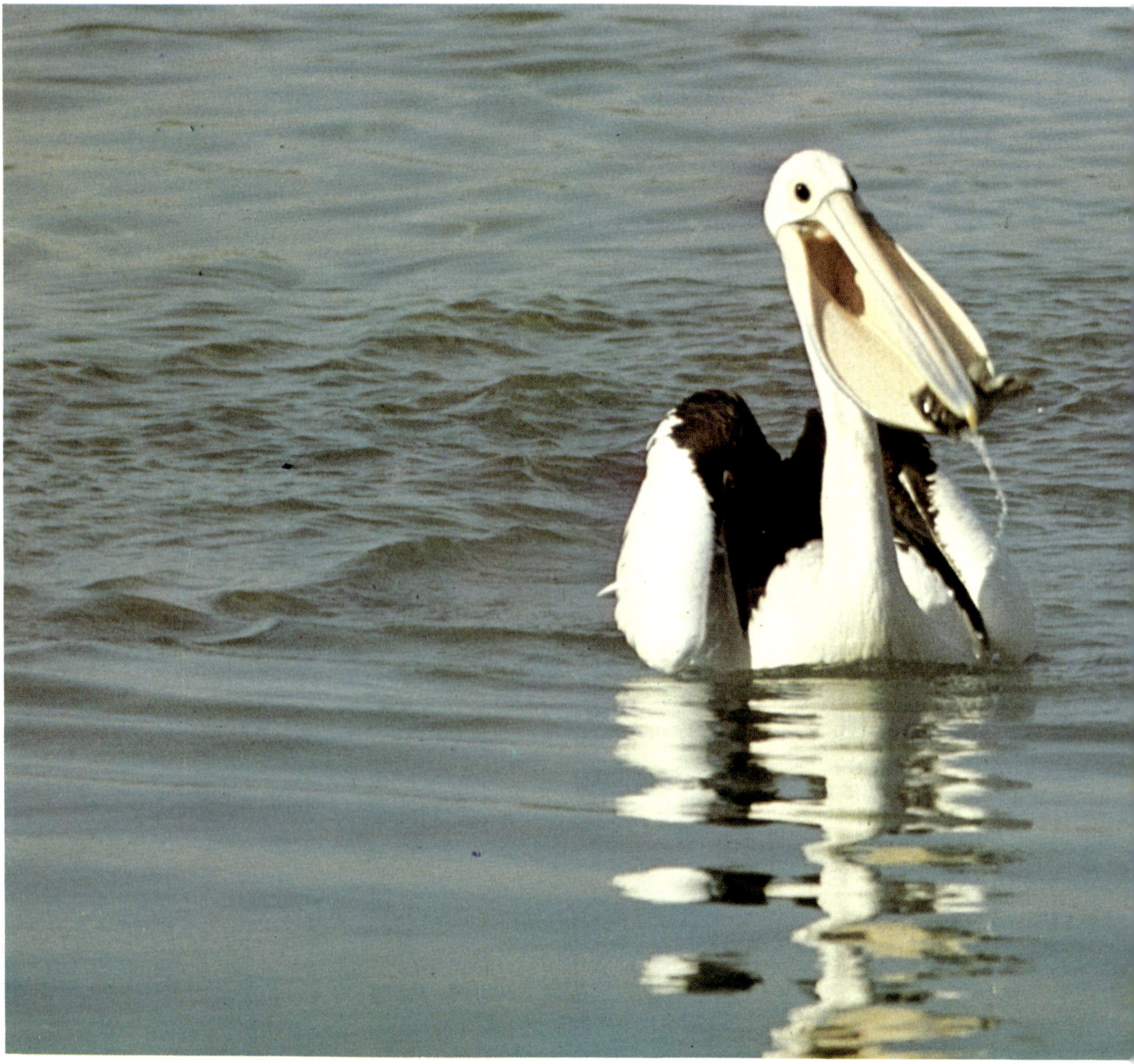

MOOLA THE PELICAN

'As a young boy, I used to sit and watch pelicans for hours. The big graceful birds would sweep down to land on the lagoons near my tribe's camp, then paddle along, dipping their large bills into the water looking for fish. Pelicans lay sometimes two, sometimes four eggs, and when the little pelicans hatch they leave their nests and spend their time playing and learning with other baby pelicans in a kind of kindergarten. One or two adults look after lots of babies while most of the adults are out looking for food. In a lot of ways they are like the Aboriginals, sharing their campsites, and the raising of their young.'

MOOLA THE PELICAN

Long ago, in the Dreamtime, there lived a pelican called Moola. In the Dreamtime pelicans were completely black, and Moola was the blackest and fiercest of them all. He was proud of the way he looked, and each day he would spend hours and hours arranging his feathers, preening and prancing, and grooming himself with his large bill.

When he was quite happy with his appearance, Moola would climb into his bark canoe and paddle around showing off to all the other birds. Moola was very proud of his canoe, because he was the only pelican who had one. The other birds would look at Moola and say,

>'Look at Moola, so proud in his canoe.'

>'I wish I had a canoe like Moola's.'

But Moola was very selfish; he would never let other pelicans ride in his canoe. When they asked, Moola would say,

>'You might fall out, canoes are difficult to paddle.'

Moola knew he looked important, sitting up in his canoe, and he didn't want the other pelicans to look important too.

One day there came a huge storm. The rain poured down, soaking all the animals. The old Wombat shivered in his hole, the Kangaroos sheltered under the trees, and still it rained. It rained so much that the rivers filled and flowed out over the land. The old Wombat knew that he would have to leave his cosy hole. As he scrambled out he saw the Kangaroos hopping off towards higher ground.

But Moola was delighted. All this water meant that he could paddle his canoe to places he had never been before! It also meant that he could show off to lots of animals who had never seen him before. Big, black, proud Moola, the only pelican with a canoe. As he paddled off, he sang,

> 'Munmuckinny, munmuckinny, munmuckinny, munmuckinny.

He hadn't rowed very far, when he came across a group of Aboriginals stranded on a tiny island. Moola could see that the rising water would soon cover the tiny island. As he came nearer he could see that there were four people; two old women, an old man and a beautiful young girl.

> 'Help, please help us. If you don't save us we will surely drown.'

The young girl, whose name was Mungi, pleaded with Moola,

*'Please save us. You have a canoe and you could
take us one at a time.'*

Moola stared at her, she was very pretty and young. And, he, Moola the proudest and blackest of all the pelicans, didn't have a woman.

Mungi felt uneasy. Why was the big, black bird staring at her like that? She huddled closer to the old woman. They were all very wet, and very frightened.

Moola stared at her. If he could get the three old people off the island, then he could come back and take the young girl for himself.

*'I will help you. Don't worry, I can save you with
my canoe. I will take you one at a time, and I will
take the oldest first.*

Moola collected the older woman and paddled her across the river to where the land was high. He helped her out of the canoe and went back again. He collected the other old woman and returned for the old man. Mungi and the old man sat huddled together on the island. Mungi was frightened. Each time Moola came to the island he stared at her and waved his big yellow bill in the air.

When the old man and Moola had gone, Mungi was left sitting all alone. She thought. She was young and very pretty, everyone told her so. Was that why Moola stared at her? She began to cry. Through the rain, she could just see the big, black bird paddling the old man towards the distant shore. She sobbed,

> *'At least the old people are safe, but I don't trust Moola. I am frightened he will steal me to be his woman.'*

Moola reached the far bank. She watched the old man climb out of the canoe. Then Moola turned to come back for Mungi. She watched as he paddled towards her. Mungi knew she must escape. If she tried to swim then Moola would only come after her. She must trick him, so that she could escape.

She had an idea. She quickly slipped the kangaroo-skin rug from around her shoulders, and she wrapped it around a log. Mungi slipped into the water and began to swim to the opposite bank.

Moola paddled up to the tiny island. He couldn't see Mungi. Where was she? He jumped out of his canoe. Mungi was nowhere to be seen. Then Moola saw the kangaroo-skin rug.

> *'That Mungi, asleep, when I Moola the most handsome of all pelicans have come to save her.'*

He rushed up to the log and gave it an almighty kick. Pain soared up his leg. He leapt into the air. He had been tricked. Mungi was gone.

Moola limped back to his canoe. No one had ever tricked him before. The more he thought of Mungi, the angrier be became.

> *'I'll go back to my camp. I'll get my spears and I'll hunt that Mungi.'*

The other pelicans saw Moola coming. He looked quite funny, paddling along with one big, swollen foot dangling out of his canoe. They began to laugh,

> *'Look at Moola.'*

> *'Moola doesn't look so important now.'*

> *'Moola, Moola, Bigfoot.'*

Their teasing only made Moola angrier. He went to his camp and splashed white war-paint over his body. The white paint made him look very fierce. Moola roared in anger, gathered his spears and started back to his canoe.

The older pelicans saw him, all covered in white war-paint. They had never seen anything like it. Pelicans, they said, should not look like this; pelicans were black. They decided to teach Moola a lesson. Flapping their wings, they rushed at him. Wheeling around him, they pecked and flapped, their huge bills plunging into Moola's black and white feathers.

When the old pelicans had finished, they told Moola that he must leave and never return. He was to be banished forever.

Although the young pelicans watched in horror as Moola stumbled away, they thought he looked very fierce and proud.

'If we painted ourselves, then we could look fierce and proud like Moola.'

So they all rushed off to paint themselves like Moola. Soon all the young pelicans in the camp had covered their black feathers with fierce blotches of white paint.

The old pelicans looked amazed. Pelicans should be black. But the young pelicans didn't listen. They went parading around, admiring their new black and white plumage.

'We look so fierce.'

'We look so proud.'

'We all look as fierce and as proud as Moola.'

And they have stayed that way ever since. And that is why, today, if you see pelicans on a lagoon or billabong, you will see that they are black with white patches, just as Moola was, long ago in the Dreamtime.

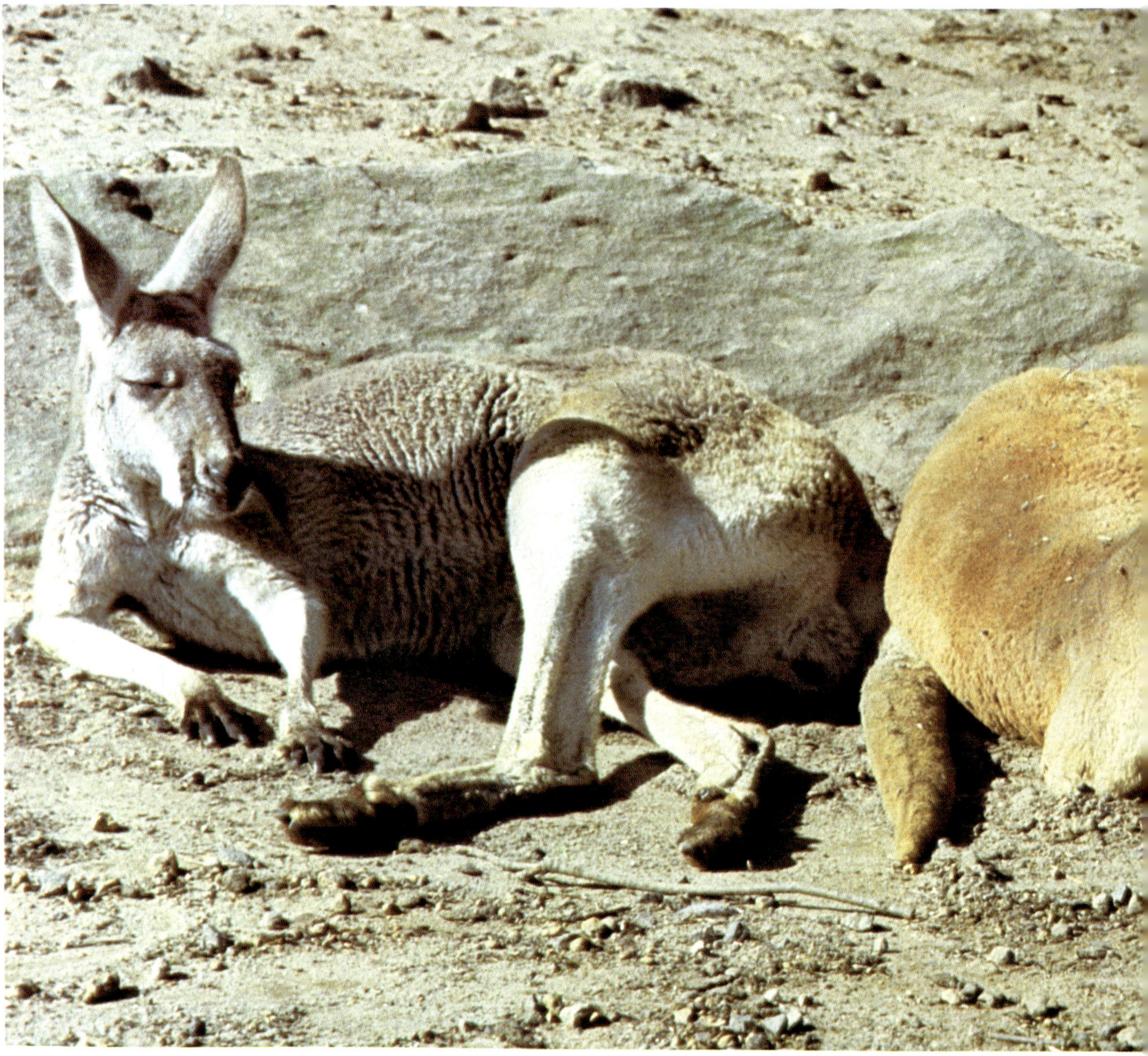

THE FIRST KANGAROOS

'Kangaroos are such funny looking animals, with their big hind legs for hopping about, and their strong tail which they use for balance — it stops them from falling over. Kangaroos, along with wallabies, goannas, barramundi fish, and fruit and vegetables, are the main things we eat. You have to be very quick to be able to sneak up and spear a kangaroo for dinner, but it tastes so nice it's well worth the effort.

The only thing is, that we all have to be careful not to kill too many kangaroos too quickly, or there won't be any left for anybody. That would be just dreadful!'

THE FIRST KANGAROOS

Long ago in the Dreamtime, there were no Kangaroos. The Aboriginals used to eat yams and fruit, and animals and fish that they hunted and trapped.

Then, one day, there came a huge storm. The wind roared and enormous trees were blown out of the ground. The wind was so strong, that it even blew possums and small animals up into the sky!

An Aboriginal tribe was camped near a billabong, when the storm broke. The huge dark clouds rolled towards them. Quickly, they took shelter in a gully. They huddled together as the storm whipped around them. Sand stung their faces, and the sky was full of leaves and branches. They had never seen a storm like it!

They were especially worried because a hunting party had gone out looking for food earlier in the day and had not yet returned. As they crouched in the gully, they hoped that their friends would be safe.

The hunting party had gone to a waterhole, where the Emus drank each afternoon. When the huge storm sprung up, they ran to hide in the rocks around the waterhole.

As the wind roared around them, they looked at the leaves and dust flying in the sky, and in this debris saw some strange creatures. The creatures were very large; they had big round hips, funny little front legs, and huge back legs that seemed to reach down to the ground. They had never seen such strange animals! Kangaroos! The Kangaroos swirled overhead, with their long legs dangling.

Suddenly, the wind dropped. The Kangaroos dropped to the ground and then slowly stood on their huge hind legs, shook themselves and hopped off into the bush.

The hunters were delighted. These were the biggest animals they had ever seen! They were sure that if they could catch one of these Kangaroos, they could feed many people.

When the wind subsided completely they set out to find their tribe. Arriving at the camp, they found nothing, for the wind had blown it away! Then they saw the smoke from the fire in the gully.

When they told the rest of the tribe about these huge creatures that hopped on big back legs, the old men of the tribe decided that they should all go and camp near the waterhole. If they could catch these Kangaroos they would all have plenty to eat.

So the next day they moved their camp to the waterhole. That afternoon, they set out to hunt the Kangaroo for the first time.

But it was a long time before the Aboriginals learned to spear the big swift creatures — the first Kangaroos.

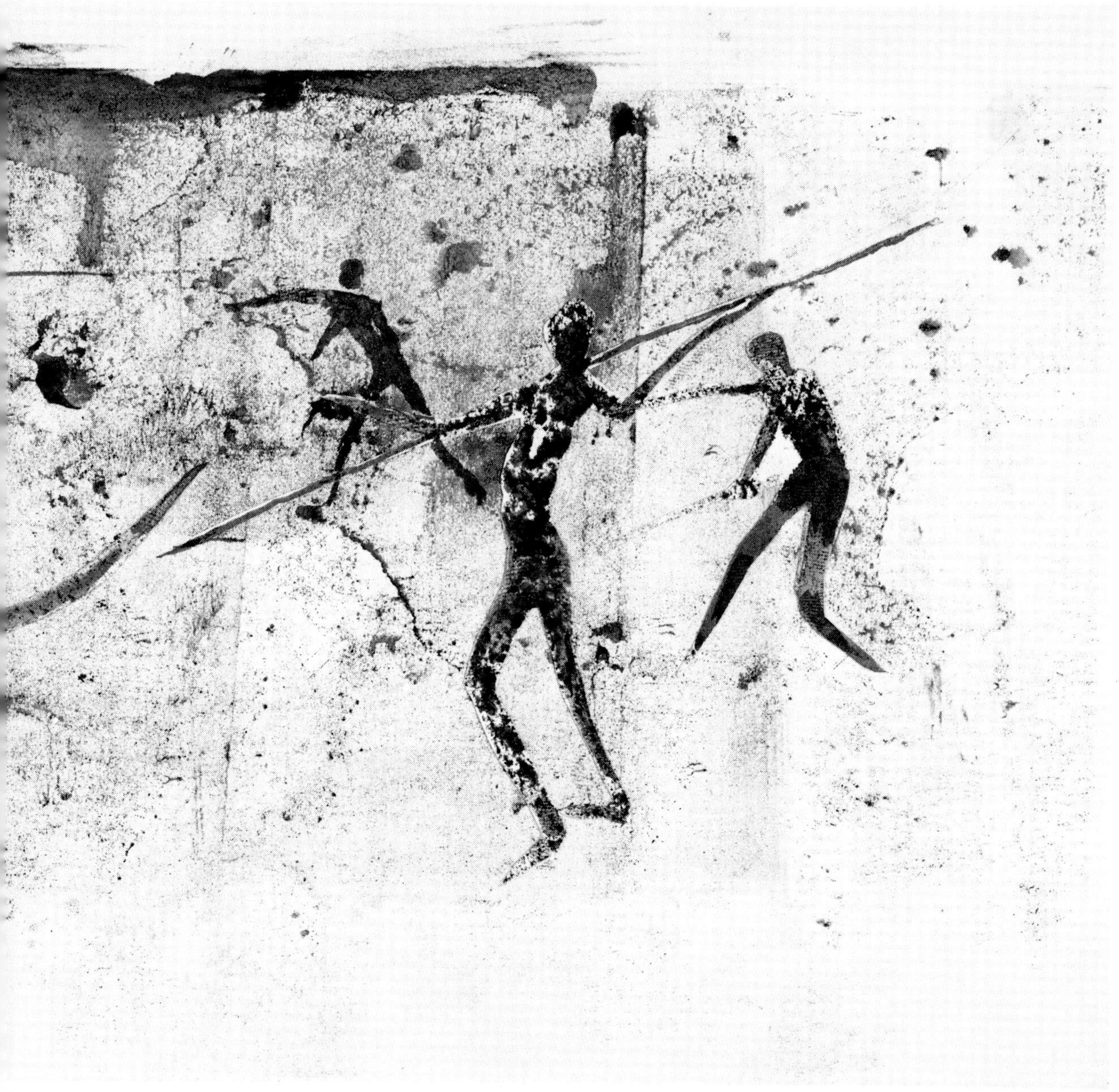

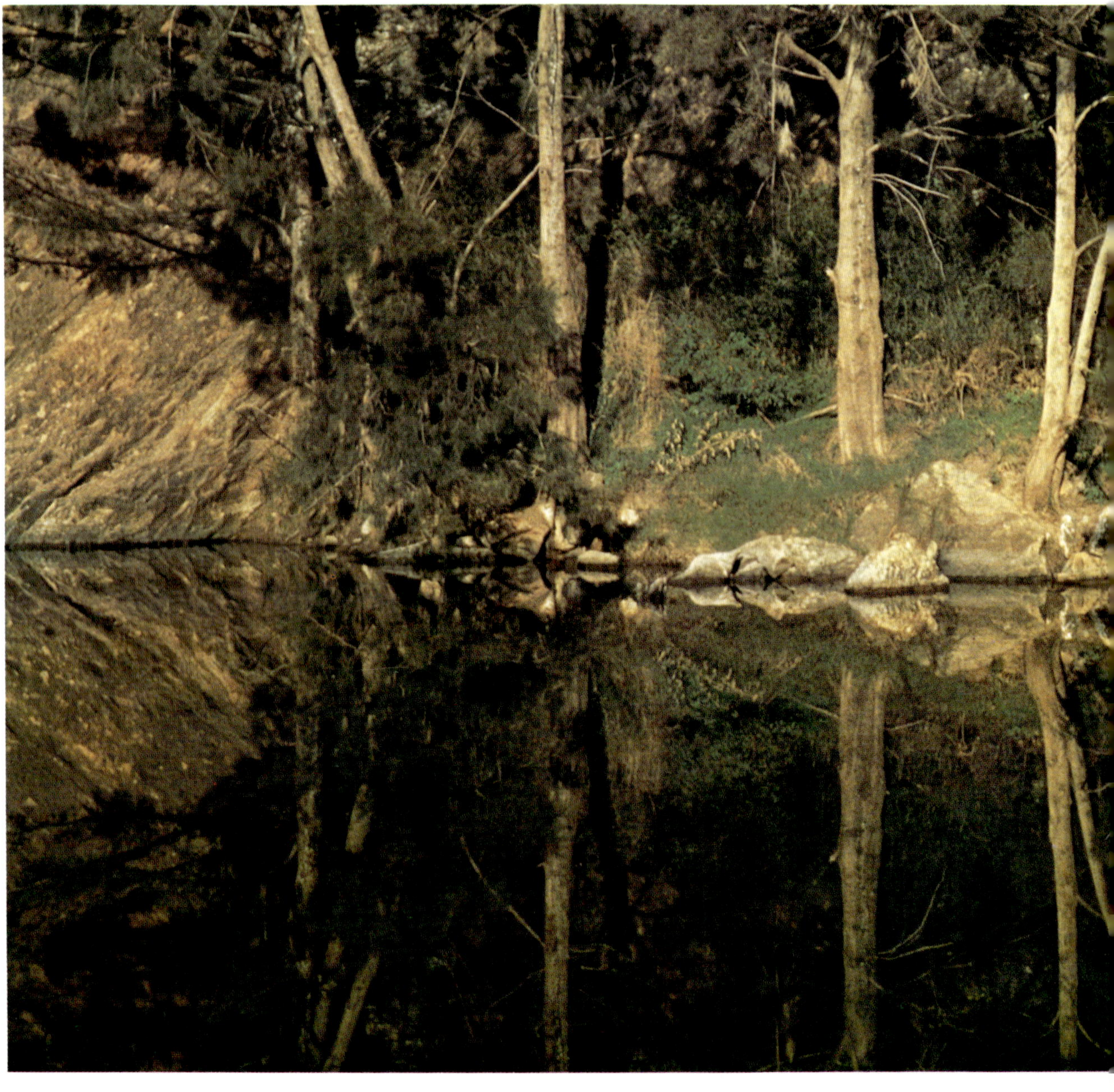

THE FIRST BARRAMUNDI FISH

Long ago in the Dreamtime there were no fish in the seas and rivers as there are today. Fortunately, in Arnhem Land where I live, there are plenty of fish — especially barramundi, the nicest fish of all.

But have you ever wondered why the fish chose to live under the water and not on the land like all the other animals and birds? The answer goes way back to the Dreamtime and to the story of two young lovers who became the first fish.

THE FIRST BARRAMUNDI FISH

Long ago in the Dreamtime there were no fish. Everyone lived on the land. There was plenty of food to eat and everyone was happy.

Except for Yungi, a young man, and Meyalk the girl he wanted to marry. They had been close friends since they were children and always played together. In fact Yungi was so much in love with Meyalk that he would not even go off into the bush to hunt, because that meant leaving her alone.

However one day Meyalk's father told Yungi that he could not marry his daughter because he was still only a boy.

> 'You are not yet even a man.'
>
> 'I'm grown up.'
>
> 'You may be, but you don't even know how to hunt. How can you be a man when you can't even throw a spear?'
>
> 'You wait, I'll soon prove to you I'm worthy of your daughter.'

And so he decided to go into the bush. He left the camp, and went off by himself, determined to stay away from all others until he had mastered spear and boomerang throwing, and could hunt his own food. He made up his mind not to come back until he was the best spear thrower and fighter in the whole land.

It took him many years to learn these skills and he was away from his tribe for a long time.

On his return he found that Meyalk's father had died, and Meyalk was now about to be given to an old man for his wife.

'She is my girl. She can't marry anyone else!'

'She has to marry the old man. He needs a young wife to look after him.'

Yungi decided to fight for his girl. He knew how to throw the spear well and he would be able to face the best fighter. But there were so many men in the tribe, and he could not fight them all. He decided to wait for a while.

That night there was a big Bora, a big corroboree. All the men of the tribe gathered in a clearing in the bush near the camp and started their singing and dancing. The best songmen and didgeridoo players were all in fine form and their music echoed through the hills and back to the camp. The only people left in the camp were the women and children who didn't take part in the Bora.

Yungi realized that here was his chance; he would get Meyalk, and together they would run away. Yungi left the Bora quietly and crept back to the camp without being noticed. He found Meyalk and off they set, slipping away into the bush.

Nobody saw them go and anyway there was no one at the camp who could chase them. But Yungi knew full well that they had broken tribal law and that they would be punished if they were caught. And soon the men from the tribe would come looking for them.

Yungi and Meyalk ran a long way; all night long they travelled, trying to cover their tracks as they went. Exhausted they reached the edge of the land where the great sea began. They could go no further. They huddled close to each other in the shelter of some rocks, alone together for the first time. But they could not sleep. Yungi knew the men would be after them.

> *'I have to make lots of spears to defend us. If I can fight them off, maybe they will leave us alone.'*
>
> *'I will help you make them!'*

Together they set about making a great many spears, tearing the straight branches from the trees, then trimming and sharpening them with the sharp stone which Yungi always carried with him in a special pouch around his arm. Soon they had gathered a pile of spears and then they built a small fire so that they could harden the points in the hot ashes.

Daybreak came, and together they watched the Sun-Woman rise up from her camp in the east and start her journey across the sky. No sooner had she risen than the first of the tribesmen appeared at the top of the rocks overlooking the shore.

As they spotted the young lovers, Yungi picked up a spear and hurled it towards them. Yungi had practised well and his spear sped straight and fast over the great distance. When the men saw the spears coming they rushed behind the rocks for shelter.

Whenever his tribesmen showed themselves from behind the rocks Yungi threw more spears, forcing them to hide again. Every time he threw a spear Meyalk would make a new one to replace it. They were able to hold the men back all day, but by the evening there was no more wood left to make the spears.

'We must run away now.'

'But we can't. The sea is behind us.'

'Without spears to defend us, the tribesmen will come down here and kill you. You stay here, I will go back to them. Then they will leave you alone.'

Yungi looked at his loved one, proud that she was prepared to give herself up to save his life.

*'No. We must stay together always. If we can't
stay here and live, then we will leave the land
and go into the sea to live.'*

Yungi, with a mighty sweep of his arm, hurled his last spear.

He then changed himself and Meyalk into two Barramundi fish. As they slid into the water together the tribesmen rushed down from the rocks hurling spears at them. Some of these struck Yungi and Meyalk, and even to this day the spikes on the back of the barramundi fish are a reminder of what happened long ago. And the fish never come out of the water on to the land for they know that death awaits them there.

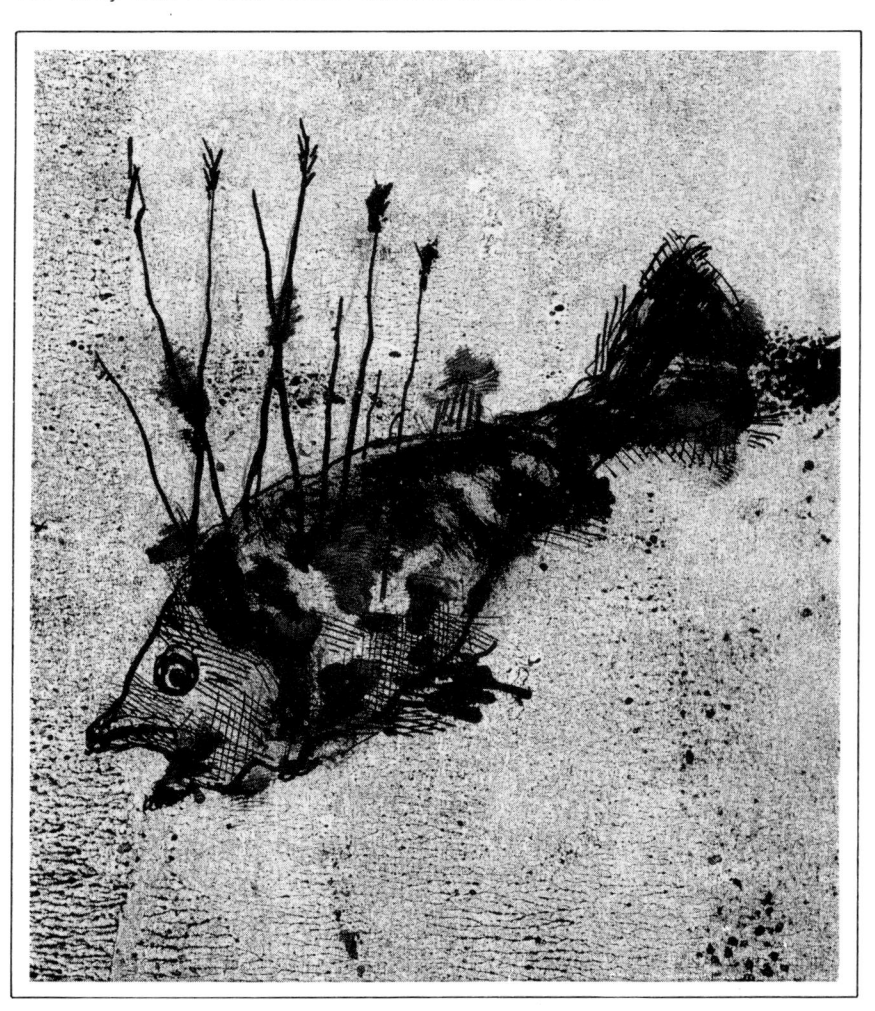

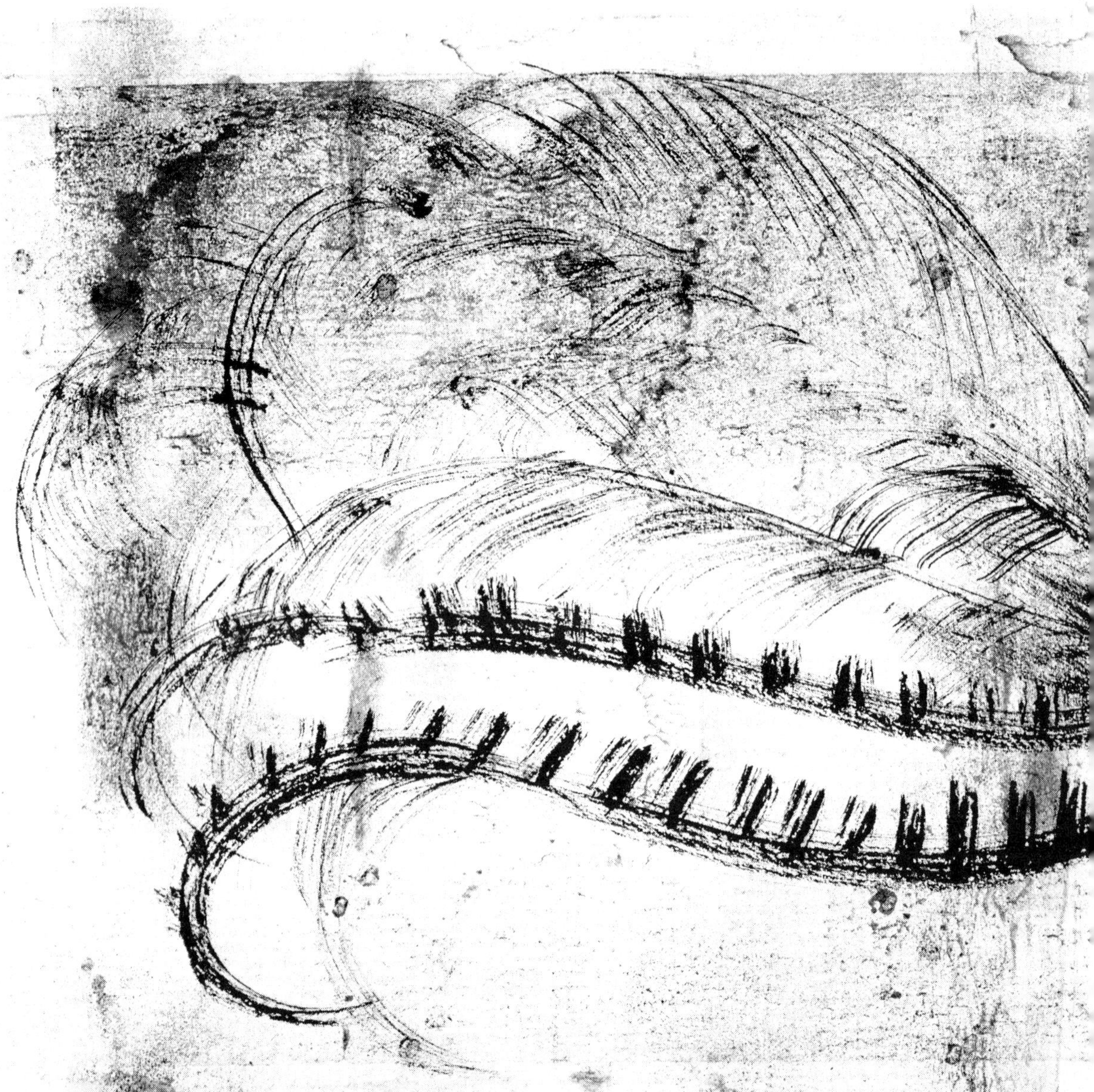

LYREBIRD THE MIMIC

'My two favourite birds are the lyrebird and the brolga. The lyrebird because of its beautiful fan-like tail, and the brolga because of its beautiful dances — and you know how much I love dancing. But the lyrebird is special for another reason. It is the only bird that is able to imitate all the other animals and birds — much better even than cockatoos or parrots! They also have a great sense of fun, and enjoy imitating our laughter — they can even imitate the sound of trees creaking in the wind!'

LYREBIRD THE MIMIC

In the Dreamtime, all the birds and animals spoke the same language. This meant that all the birds and animals could talk to each other, and understand each other, and there were no fights. There was plenty of food to eat, and at this time no animal ever hunted another. They had nothing to fear. Even the tiny Whip Snake and the Kookaburra were friends.

One day, all the animals and the birds decided that they would hold a huge corroboree, with lots of singing and dancing. The corroboree was to last for several days, so a great quantity of food was collected, and all the animals and birds in the whole land were to attend.

The Brolga, being the best dancing bird in the land, was to be in charge of the dancing, and the Dingo and Kookaburra were going to sing. Everyone was looking forward to it.

On the day it was to start, all the animals began to gather at the waterhole near the camp of the Lyrebird. The Native Cat, slinking in from the bush, was the first to arrive, and then the Crows, the Eagles, the Galahs and the Magpie Geese flew in. The old Wombat waddled in, the Kangaroo and the Wallaby hopped in together, and the Frog arrived with the Platypus. It was the largest gathering anyone could remember.

They set up their camps, and readied themselves for the corroboree. It was a splendid affair. Never before had they enjoyed themselves so much. The Kookaburra told some jokes, and laughed much louder than anyone else!

The Frog, who was the greatest mimic in the whole land, then copied the Kookaburra's voice, and told some more stories. All the animals, even the Kookaburra, roared laughing. They all agreed that the Frog was certainly a very clever mimic.

Then the Brolga danced, and all the animals and birds joined in, even the old Wombat. The Frog thought that the Wombat looked so funny, dancing beside the graceful Brolga.

Then the Frog had an idea. He would really have some fun! He copied the Brolga's voice, and called out to the Wombat,

> *'You look so stupid! Fancy a fat little roly-poly like you, trying to dance!'*

The Wombat stopped and looked at the Brolga. No one had ever been rude to him before! Not even the nasty Crows.

The Frog, seeing how well his trick had worked, took on the voice of the Brolga, and called out to the Emu,

'Hey, Emu, why are you trying to dance. Emus can't dance, they can't even fly!'

The Emu was furious. No one had ever teased her about her small wings before. The Emu ran towards the Brolga.

The Frog, thinking that this was great fun, began calling out all sorts of rude remarks. He imitated the Kangaroo and the Kookaburra; he insulted the Platypus, who thought it was the Eagle being nasty. Soon all the animals at the corroboree were hurling insults at each other. And in the middle, sat the Frog. He was having great fun. There were animals and birds quarrelling and fighting all around him.

Then the Frog, using the voice of the Wombat, yelled,

'To battle! Let's fight! Come on, to battle!'

A huge fight broke out, and as the animals fought, the Frog hopped quietly up on to a high rock, to watch the whole fight.

Only the Lyrebird took no part in the fight. Fanning his beautiful tail feathers, he went from quarrel to quarrel, pleading with the animals to stop.

But stop they wouldn't! The Kookaburra was fighting with the Whip Snake. The Crows were chasing a Lizard.

The Lyrebird pleaded,

> 'Please, please stop! We are all friends. It is senseless to fight. Please stop!'

But no one took any notice of the Lyrebird. In fact the fighting grew even worse! The noise was deafening. Shouts and groans filled the air. The Frog was jumping around on his rock, yelling more insults, urging on the fighting.

Now, the noise of all this woke the Spirits. Seeing what had happened, they became so annoyed that they put an end to the battle.

The animals were very embarrassed. They had never fought before. To punish them, the Spirits took away the creatures' common language, and gave each animal and bird a language of its own. The wicked Frog, who had the most beautiful voice, was given an ugly croak as punishment for having started the fight.

The Lyrebird, the only animal who had tried to stop the fighting, was rewarded by the Spirits. They decided that from this time, the Lyrebird was to be the only animal who would be able to talk to all other animals.

Even to this day, the lyrebird is the only animal that is able to imitate all other animals. And to this day Aboriginal people have a special respect for lyrebirds because of their role as peacemakers. Today, frogs still talk in an ugly croak. And still today, no animal or bird can talk to a different animal or bird. They can only talk with their own kind.

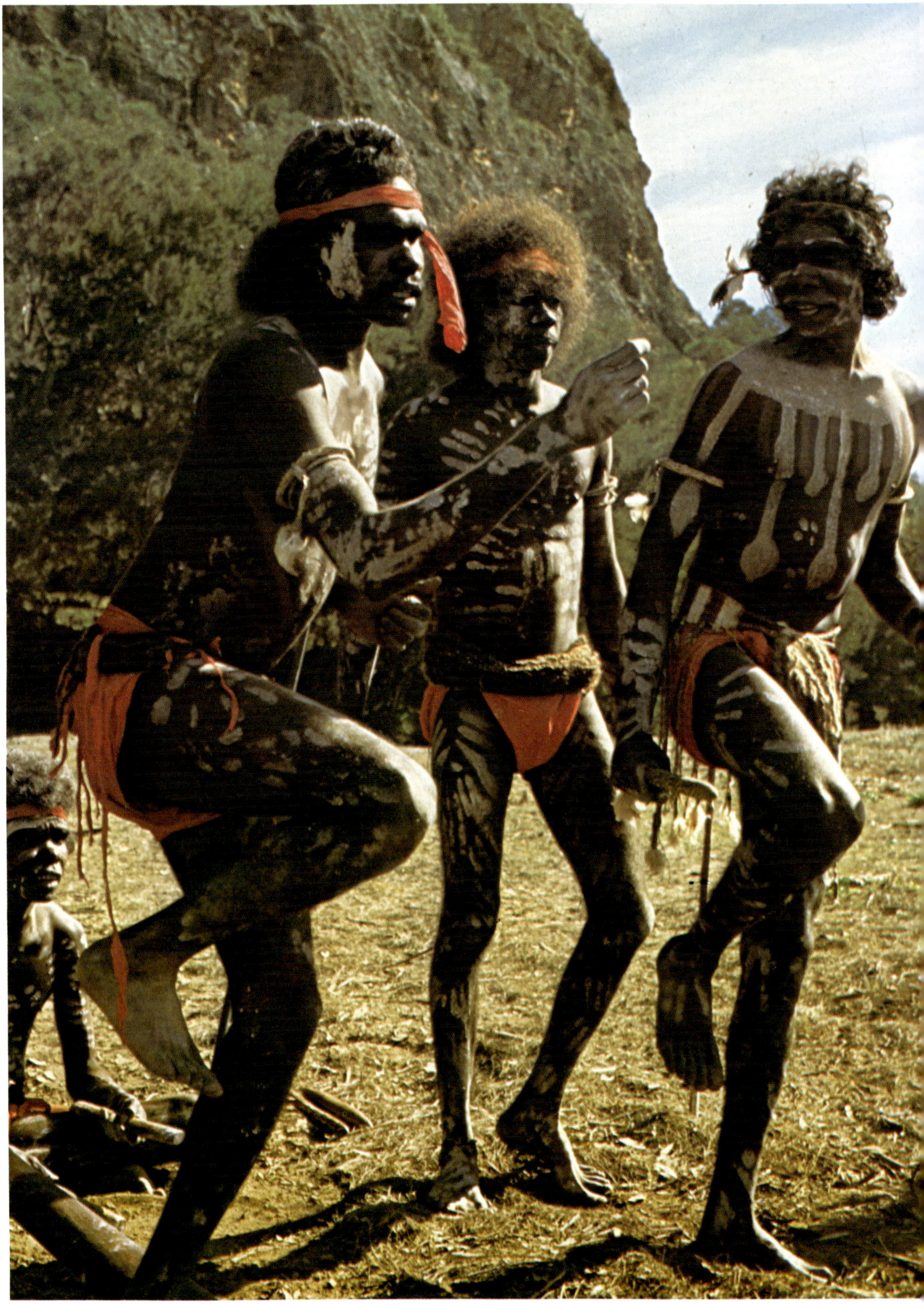

EMU & WILD TURKEY

'Many people know that the emu is the fastest runner in the bird world. I can't catch them just by running — they always get away. But if you're clever you can sneak up close or else trick them and then you can catch them.

And did you know that they whistle as they run? It's quite a loud whistle and helps the young ones to follow their parents when they are going really fast.

We rarely hunt emus as their meat is a bit tough, but if we catch one we always pull out a few feathers from its tail and wear them for our corroborees and ceremonies.'

EMU & WILD TURKEY

Long ago in the Dreamtime, the Emu and the wild Turkey were sisters. As children, they went everywhere together, they played, hunted and danced together, and they sang through the gullies and the bush.

Boarta the Turkey was older than Wooripun the Emu. Because she was older, she always told the stories of their adventures. Emu didn't seem to mind. She was taller, and could run faster, and fly higher than all the other birds. Because the Emu was the larger and faster of the two, she was the queen of all the birds. But as the days passed, and the sisters grew older, so they grew apart.

One day as Boarta the Turkey was gathering food near the river, she saw her sister flying high above her. Wooripun the Emu was twirling and whirling, and because Boarta the Turkey knew that her sister was showing off, she said,

> 'Just because she has bigger wings than I, it doesn't make her the queen of all the birds.'

One day, Turkey was returning to her camp with some fish that her friend Pelican had just caught. Turkey loved fish, and thought that it was very good of Pelican to give them to her.

As she approached her camp, her sister Wooripun came parading past. When Emu saw the fish, she stopped.

> 'Fish! Oh, how I do love fish! They are my favourite food in all the land! Are you going to share them with me?

Turkey was furious! Here was her sister whom she now hated, asking for her share of fish! Wooripun would have to be taught a lesson. One she would never forget! So Boarta lied to her sister.

> 'If you like fish, why don't you catch them yourself? I do. It's really very easy. And anyway, you can only eat fish if you catch them yourself. Otherwise, a bone will catch in your throat, and will choke you!'

Wooripun the Emu thought that this sounded a bit silly. But her sister was older, and knew more than she did, so what she said must be right.

The Emu followed Turkey back to her camp, her eyes never leaving the fish in the dilli bag. Then Turkey sat down, and began to eat. She didn't offer Emu any, but ate it all by herself, saying,

> 'Fish is such lovely food. I don't know what I
> would do if I couldn't catch fish!'

Emu sat and watched. She was very hungry. So she said to her sister,

> 'Will you teach me to catch fish? I know I could if
> you showed me how.'

The Turkey finished eating, and agreed to show Emu how to catch fish.

> 'I am one of the best fishermen in the whole
> land. I am good because my wings are small. You
> couldn't fish with those big clumsy wings of
> yours.'

Wooripun the Emu looked at her sister Boarta's wings. They were small, and fitted snugly against her body. Turkey told her that if she wanted to be a good fisherman, she would have to cut off her beautiful big wings!

*'Cut off my wings? But I need my wings for my
long journeys. How will I fly without them?'*

So Boarta the Turkey told her that it would be really simple to cut them off, and then if she ever needed them, they could always be stuck on again. And what was more, without her wings, the Emu could catch all the fish she ever wanted.

Emu could resist no longer. She loved fish, so her wings would have to come off. And, as Turkey said, she could always have them back when she wanted them. Turkey would arrange the ceremony for cutting her sister's wings.

All the animals gathered for the ceremony. The old Wombat brought the special stone for Wooripun to use. Emu was ready. She could almost taste the fish! As soon as her wings were gone, she would rush to the river, and begin to fish.

The animals formed a circle and Emu stood in the centre. With two quick blows with the special stone, Turkey cut her sister's wings off!

The animals had never seen an Emu with no wings. She did look a bit silly! They began to giggle. Emu just stood there. What were they laughing at? Was it her? Then she realized. It was her! They were laughing at her! She looked down at her beautiful wings, lying on the ground. Turkey had tricked her. She would never fly again.

The animals rolled about laughing. That would teach Emu that she wasn't queen of the birds! Poor Emu, she wanted to die. She stumbled away into the bush to hide her shame. She would never forgive her sister.

A long time passed before the sisters met again. By then, the Emu had ten children. One day, she was out hunting with two of her children when she saw her sister Turkey in the distance. Emu put her head in the air and started to hurry off, but Turkey, who had seen her, called out to her,

*'Sister, how does it feel to be queen of the birds,
and have no wings?'*

Emu stopped. The words stung her. She looked at Turkey, and then at her ten children. Emu was wingless, but she would have her revenge somehow.

She said to Turkey,

*'I feel for you. I have forgiven you your mean
deed. Now I have these two lovely children to
comfort me. But I feel sorry for you.'*

This surprised Boarta the Turkey. Why should the Emu forgive her? Emu explained to her sister,

> 'Look at your children. You have so many, and they are so small. Do they get enough to eat? Look at my two. They are big and strong, but then I have only two children, and you have ten. Oh, I do feel sorry for you!'

Turkey looked at Wooripun the Emu's two children. Indeed, they were big and strong. Turkey hated to think that her little sister would have bigger and stronger children than she. While she was wondering what to do, Emu called out,

> 'I know what I would do. I'd pick out the healthiest two, and keep them. Then I would kill all the rest, so they are not a disgrace to you.'

Turkey said nothing. She gathered up her children, and walked away. Perhaps Emu was right, perhaps her children were not eating enough.

The next day, Wooripun the Emu and two of her children were feeding at the waterhole again. They hadn't been there long when Turkey arrived with only two of her children. Emu looked at them.

> 'What happened to the rest of your poor starving children? Did you leave them at your camp?'

Turkey spread her wings, gave a little flap, and said to her sister,

> 'I have killed them. Now my two children will grow up to be as big and strong as yours are. Now we will have children of the same size, but I will still have my wings.'

Emu gave a little low whistle, and as she did so, eight little striped feathered chicks ran from the bush, and joined their mother.

Turkey let out a cry. She had been tricked into killing eight of her children. Then Wooripun the Emu said to her,

> 'You have your wings, and I have all my children. You tricked me because you were jealous. I lost my wings because I was greedy. Now I have tricked you, and your envy has cost you eight of your children. Let us stop now, and live our lives in peace.'

And ever since that time, the emu has had no wings, and the wild turkey has only laid two eggs, a permanent reminder of their greed and jealousy, long ago in the Dreamtime.

We have a legend that explains the formation of the hills, the rivers and all the shapes of the land. Every time it rains and I see a beautiful rainbow I am reminded of the legend of the Rainbow Serpent.

THE RAINBOW SERPENT

Long long ago in the Dreamtime a group of Aboriginals were out hunting for wallabies. It had been raining and the ground was soft making it hard for them to run. The wallabies, feeling refreshed by the rain, were flighty and difficult to stalk. The Aboriginals came to a clump of trees near the edge of a small plain, and there they decided to rest.

As they sat around, telling stories and warming their hands by the fire, one of them looked up. There on the horizon was a beautiful multi-coloured arch. A rainbow.

'Look, look, over there.'

'There goes the Rainbow Serpent. He is moving from his old waterhole to another.'

They were a little fearful. They did not want the huge, brightly-coloured Serpent in a waterhole near their camp. They were grateful that he did not seem to be moving too near their own waterhole. They sat and talked some more, mostly about the Rainbow Serpent, but also about hunting and fishing, and about the battles they had fought.

One young man, Bandalil, kept wanting to know more about the Rainbow Serpent. The other hunters laughed at him.

'Little Bandilil, be patient. You'll find out about the Rainbow Serpent. What's the hurry?'

But Bandalil said he wanted to find out more about the Rainbow Serpent and threatened to set off for the waterhole, where it now lived. The others pleaded with him.

'Don't go. You mustn't disturb the Rainbow Serpent.'

'Don't go, Bandalil. It'll only cause trouble.'

So Bandalil agreed to wait and ask the old men of the tribe about the Serpent.

When the hunting party returned to their camp, the children ran out to greet them. Even though they had caught only two wallabies, not really enough for everyone, there would be singing and dancing, a big corroboree, that night.

During the corroboree, Bandalil went over to where the old men were sitting.

'Tell me about the Rainbow Serpent. If everyone is so frightened of him I will go and spear him, then no one need fear any more.'

The old men were horrified. The Rainbow Serpent was one of the Dreamtime creatures who had shaped the earth. In the beginning the earth was flat, a vast grey plain. As the Rainbow Serpent wound his way across the land, the movement of his body heaped up the mountains and dug troughs for the rivers. With each thrust of his huge multi-coloured body, a new landform was created. He was the biggest of the Dreamtime Beings. Even the other Dreamtime creatures thought that he looked enormous, and they were very careful to leave him alone.

At last, tired with the effort of shaping the earth, he crawled into a waterhole. The cool water washed over his vast body, cooling and soothing him. The other animals watched as the water blurred the bright colours of his body. Then he sank from sight.

Each time the animals visited the waterhole, they were careful not to disturb the Rainbow Serpent, for although they could not see him they knew he was there. Then one day, after a heavy rainstorm, they saw him. His huge coloured body was arching up from the waterhole, over the tree-tops, up through the clouds, across the plain to another waterhole.

To this day the Aboriginals are careful not to disturb the Rainbow Serpent, as they see him going across the sky, from one waterhole to another.

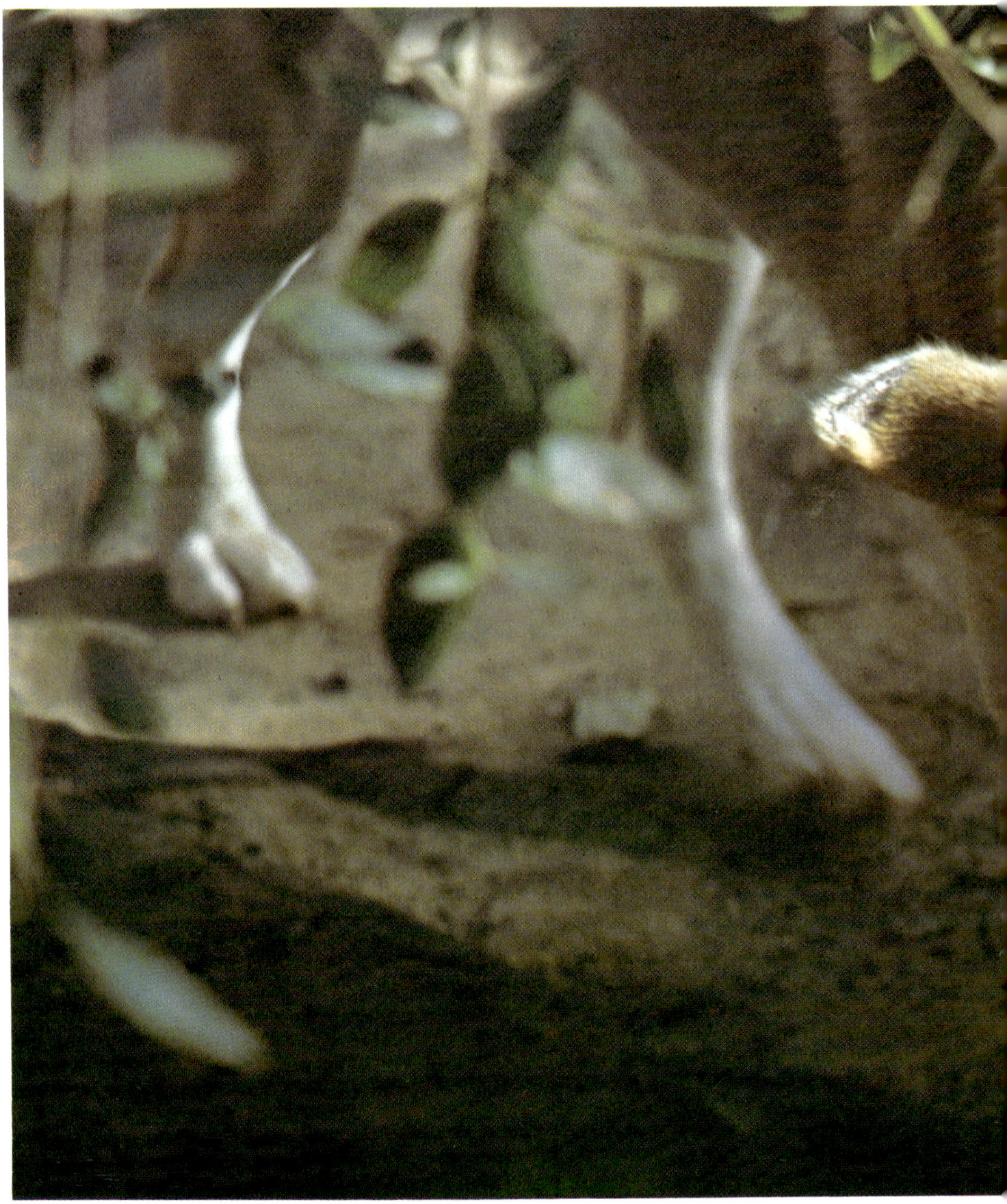

OLD YIRBAIK-BAIK & HER DINGOES

'Apparently, we are the only country in the world to have dingoes — which look like big dogs. They can be quite fierce, but they are also good friends to us, and help us in our hunting. And they guard the camp too.

Here's a really frightening legend about a wicked old woman and her dingoes who did terrible things to my people long ago.'

OLD YIRBAIK·BAIK & HER DINGOES

Yirbaik-baik was a very old woman who lived long ago in the Dreamtime. She was so old that she couldn't dig for yams or gather berries, and she lived all alone with a pack of Dingoes for her friends. But she was no ordinary old woman. She had trained her Dingoes to catch people, and she and her Dingoes lived by eating the flesh of other Aboriginals.

Yirbaik-baik had been with Dingoes ever since they were very young, and she had trained them to be very cunning and very fierce.

The dogs and the old woman would spend their days roaming the bush, hunting for people. And Yirbaik-baik and her Dingoes were such clever hunters, that they rarely went hungry.

They would sneak through the bush until they found someone who had wandered away from a hunting party, and then set a trap for them. Yirbaik-baik would hobble towards the unfortunate person, calling in a trembling voice,

> 'I am old. I am old. Can you help me? My legs are tired, and I cannot walk much further.'

As their victim came to help the old woman, the dogs would rush out of the bushes, and leap onto them.

One day, Yirbaik-baik and her Dingoes were out hunting. All day they looked, wandering in the hot sun, creeping up over hills, but they had found nothing. They were very tired and very hungry. The Dingoes began to worry. It was two days since their last meal, and their ribs were beginning to show. Yirbaik-baik suggested they rest in the shade of a big old coolibah tree. The Dingoes flopped in the shade. After wandering all day, it was pleasant to have a break.

> 'Yirbaik-baik, Yirbaik-baik. If we don't find something soon, we shall have to spend the night here. Let's start back to our camp. We can hunt again in the morning.'

Even old Yirbaik-baik had begun to think they should go back. She decided to have one last try.

> 'You wait here, while I go and look from the top of that hill. If I can see nothing, then we will all go home. But I am so hungry that it will not be an easy night.'

The Dingoes settled down to wait as the old woman hobbled off.

When she got near the top of the small hill, Yirbaik-baik fell down on her hands and knees, and began crawling. If there was anyone, she certainly didn't want them to see her. As she pushed through the grass on the top of the hill, she saw down below a small hunting party of about ten men. The hunters carried spears over their shoulders, woomeras and coolamongs in their hands. Just what she'd been looking for!!

Yirbaik-baik crawled back over the hill, and signalled to her Dingoes. They knew what they had to do. Then she stood up, put on her best old, old woman's face, and hobbled down towards the hunting party.

When the hunting party saw her, they stopped. What was an old woman doing here, all alone?

> 'Hello, old woman.'

> 'Hello. What are you hunting for?'

> 'Wallabies, goannas, anything — food is so scarce.'

Then the old woman told the hunting party that she had seen some wallabies not far away, just over the hill.

> 'I am too weak and old to hunt, but if you share with me, then I will help you get them.'

The hunting party listened to the old woman's plan. They were to go to the other side of the hill, and wait while the old woman crept around behind the wallabies. She would then scare them up to the hunting party.

It seemed a good idea, so they agreed, thanking the old woman for her offer of help. So Yirbaik-baik went off through the bush, and the hunting party gathered their spears, and boomerangs and went over the hill, to wait for the wallabies.

As they waited, they heard strange noises.

> *'Ssh! That will be the wallabies and the old woman. Ready now!'*

Then suddenly, the hungry Dingoes burst through the bush, and fell on the hunting party, killing them all. Yirbaik-baik and the Dingoes took the bodies back to their camp, and ate them.

That night, when the hunting party did not return to their camp, the rest of the tribe began to worry. They could not be lost — this was their own land! What could have happened? They decided to wait until morning and then go and look for them.

At dawn the next day, the men of the tribe gathered. They would send out a large hunting party, and some of the children could go too, so they could learn to hunt, and follow tracks.

After they had been looking for most of the morning, they came across a hidden gully. It was surrounded by large coolibah trees and lots of scrub and grass. And in the middle of the gully, there was Yirbaik-baik's camp. They crept slowly up to the camp, but no one was there. Then they saw the bones of their friends, strewn about under the trees and behind rocks.

The hunting party realized what had happened. But who would have killed their friends and eaten them? They decided to wait in hiding and find out.

Later that day, Yirbaik-baik and her Dingoes, tired from hunting, came back to the camp. Yirbaik-baik hobbled along at the front, and all her Dingoes, heads down, panted along behind her. They would be pleased to get back to their camp in the gully.

The hunting party waited until they were almost in the middle of the gully. Then with fearsome yells and shouts, they fell on Yirbaik-baik, and her Dingoes, killing them.

As each Dingo died it changed into a brown Tiger Snake, and slithered into the bush.

When Yirbaik-baik died, she too changed. She became a small brown bird, the Lidji-Lidji, and ran off into the bush. And the skulls of the dead around Yirbaik-baik's camp changed slowly into small white boulders, and their bones became bleached pieces of wood.

The Lidji-Lidji bird wasn't seen for a long time, and it is still very rare today. Now, sometimes, if you are very careful, you may see this bird, and at night you may hear its whistling, warbling call. Calling, calling, just as long ago in the Dreamtime, Yirbaik-baik called to her Dingoes.

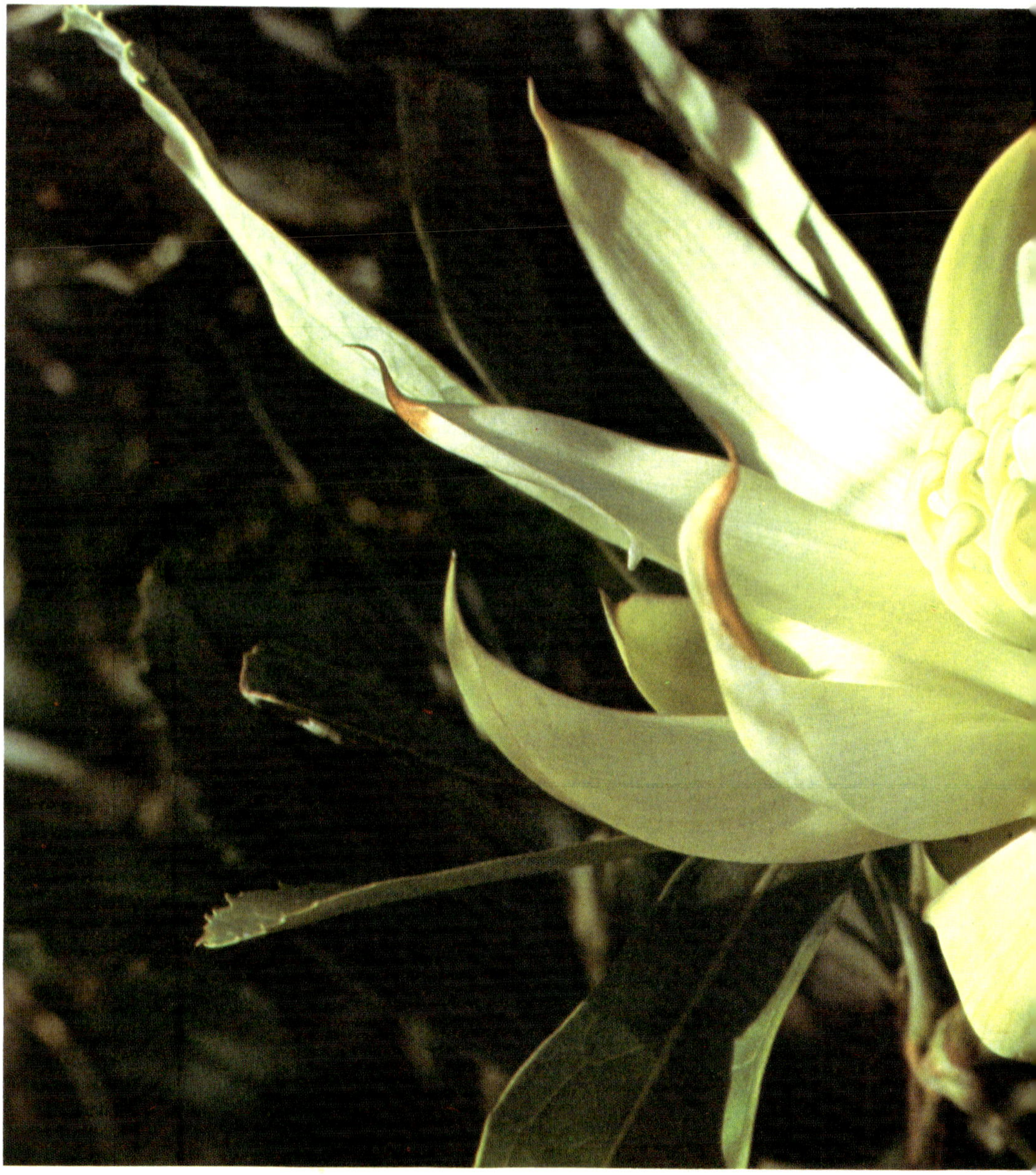

WONGA PIGEON & THE WHITE WARATAH

'Wonga pigeons are a bit like ordinary pigeons, but they live out in the bush, and hunt for food on the forest floor. Sometimes, you can see a pair of them together, resting near a beautiful flower called the waratah. There is a reason for the Wonga pigeons liking the waratah, and it goes way back into the Dreamtime.

Waratah flowers are nearly always red, but if you search very carefully, you can sometimes find a white one, hidden in the bush. This is a sad legend of the Wonga pigeon and that beautiful flower.'

WONGA PIGEON & THE WHITE WARATAH

Long ago in the Dreamtime, there were many wonderful plants and flowers, just as there are now. Some of them today are just as they were in the Dreamtime, but some have changed. The waratah flower is one of these.

The waratah is an unusual flower, because it grows at the top of a sturdy stem that reaches out of a small bush. Usually the flower is a deep red, but occasionally, a white one may be found. However, in the Dreamtime, all the waratahs were white.

In those days, the Wonga Pigeon used to live in the bushland with her mate, Lapara. They would spend their time on the floor of the forest, searching for seeds, or wandering among the trees, looking for berries.

The Wonga Pigeon had to stay below the trees, for although she could fly, she was never brave enough to fly above the tree-tops. She knew that the clear sky, up above the trees, was the land of the Hawk, the deadly enemy of the Wonga Pigeon.

One day, Wonga and Lapara were out looking for berries, when they became separated. Wonga called out,

> 'Coo-coo, coo-coo. Lapara, can you hear me? Can you hear me?'

She listened, but there was no reply. Wonga sat and waited. This had never happened before, where could her mate have gone? She called again and again, but there was no reply. She waited until the day was nearly over, and then she decided to fly off to search for him.

She flew from tree to tree, calling as she went, but there was no reply. It was getting late, and it would soon be too dark to continue.

Wonga decided that the only hope of finding her mate before dark would be to fly above the trees. She had never flown above the tree-tops before, but she thought it would be so much easier to find Lapara if she was up high. She was so worried that she didn't even think of the Hawks that lived in the sky above.

Wonga flew towards the tree-tops. Higher and higher she flew. Up past the tallest branches, and then out into the clear blue sky. She had never seen the tops of the trees before. They stretched out before her, a wrinkled and lumpy field of grey-green. Wonga sang through the sky, her little wings tugging at the air. It was a joy to be out! Had she not been worried about her mate, Wonga would have liked to float about, enjoying this new world.

As she flew about, she kept calling,

'Lapara, where are you? Where are you? Please answer me. Can you hear me calling?'

She heard a call from way down beneath her. Wonga gave a happy little flap, and turned towards it. She had found her mate!

Then she heard a strange sound. The sound of wind rushing through trees, but it seemed to come from above her. She looked up. It was a Hawk! He had seen her, and was hurtling down, his wings tucked back, his strong beak breaking the air.

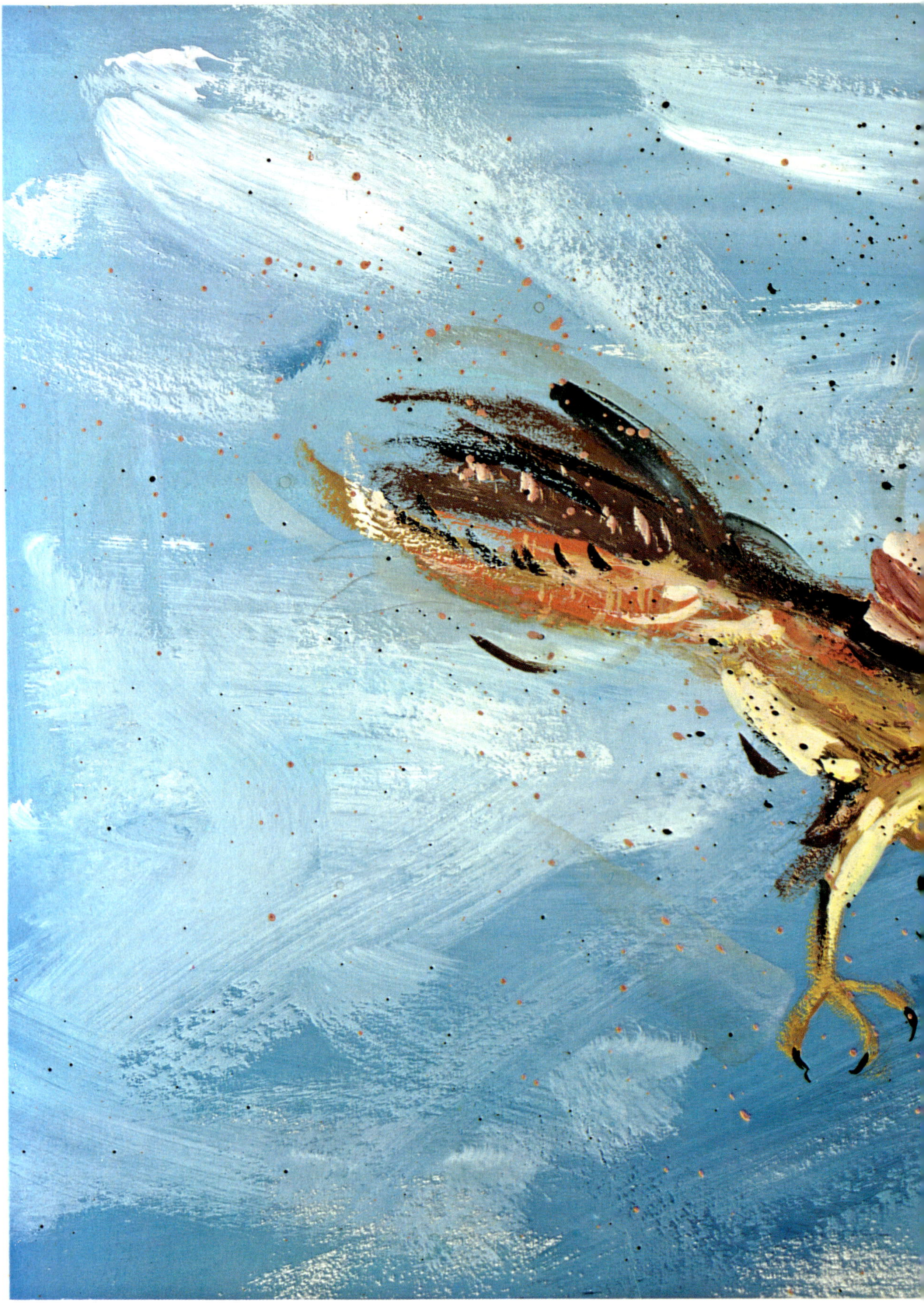

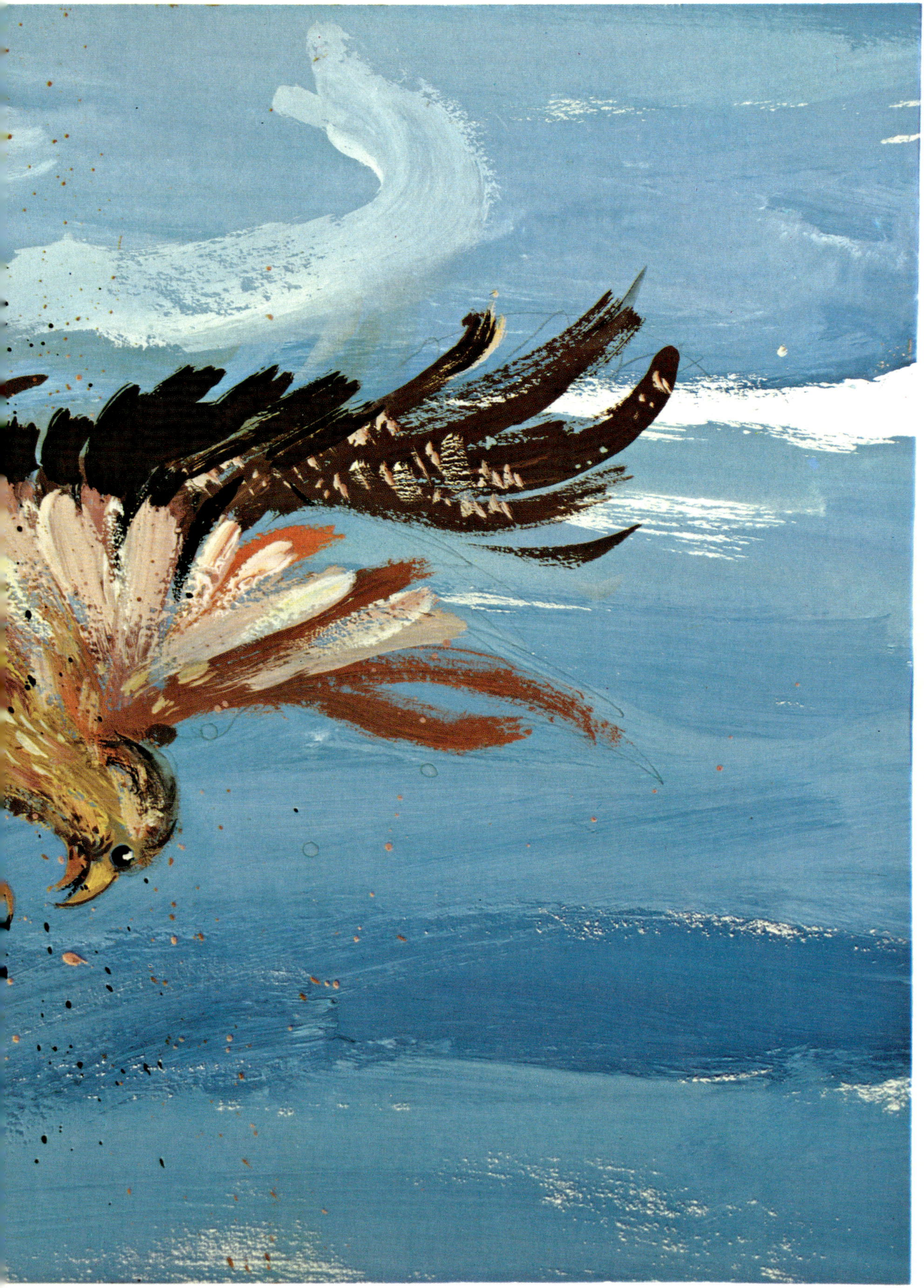

Wonga madly flapped her tiny wings, trying in a desperate panic to reach the trees. Then a searing pain struck her, as the Hawk sank his great brown talons into her body. Wonga felt all her breath go. The Hawk's crushing grip tightened. Wonga felt her breast tear open, as the Hawk hauled her upward.

Far below, she could hear Lapara calling, very faintly,

'Wonga, Wonga, where are you? Wonga, where are you?'

With a desperate effort, she tore herself free from the Hawk, and plunged downwards, into the forest below. Unable to fly, she crashed through the tree-tops, and bleeding and broken, she landed in a patch of waratah bushes. She could see the Hawk circling way above, but she was safe now, beneath the trees.

Wonga could hear her mate calling,

> 'Wonga, where are you? Where are you, Wonga?'

Pain shot through her broken body. Her blood trickled down onto one of the white waratah flowers. Wonga fluttered her wings. She must reach Lapara. Straining with all her energy, Wonga tried to fly. She managed to go only a short distance, and then she fell onto another waratah bush. Once more she tried to fly, only to land on another waratah bush. As she rested, her blood trickled down on to the waratahs, staining the flowers a deep red.

At last, exhausted and dying, she felt the last of her energy leave her. She fell softly onto the leafy forest floor, where she died. The voice of her mate still called in vain,

'Wonga, Wonga, coo-coo, coo-coo.'

This is why today, most waratah flowers are red, coloured by the blood of the Wonga Pigeon as, long ago, she flew from flower to flower in search of her mate. Sometimes, although it is very rare, it is still possible to find a white waratah, just as they were back in the Dreamtime.

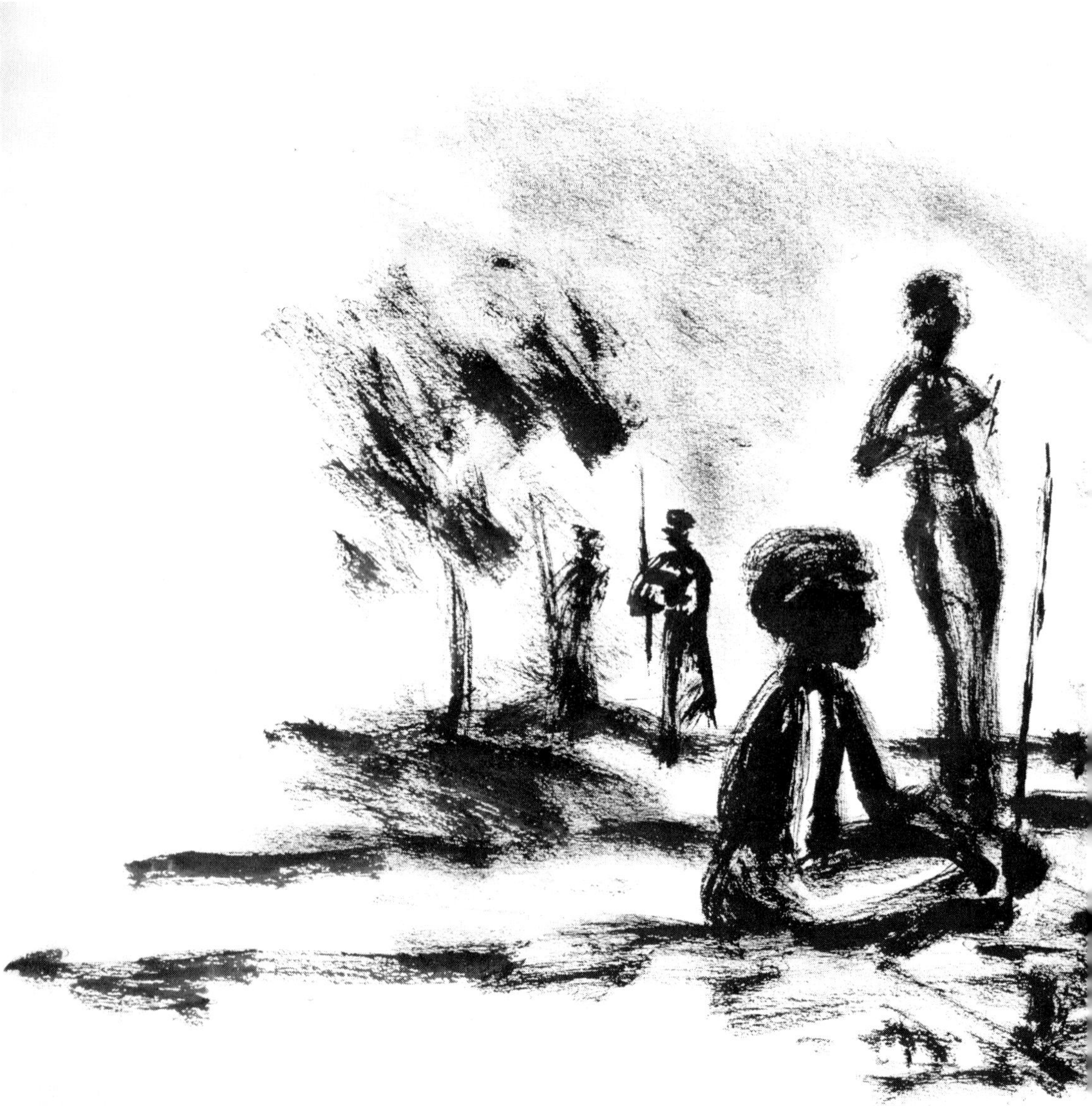

THE BIRTH OF THE BUTTERFLIES

'When spring comes around, I often see great numbers of butterflies flying round my homeland. As a young boy, I used to wonder where they all came from, so very suddenly. Then one day a wise elder of my tribe told me this legend, which explains that a butterfly is really a caterpillar, reborn into a beautiful new shape. This is what we believe happens to us when we die too — our soul is reborn again into a different body.'

THE BIRTH OF THE BUTTERFLIES

Long ago in the Dreamtime, when the world was very young, all the birds and animals spoke the same language. So the Kookaburra could talk to the Wombat, and the Wombat to the Emu, and the Eagle to the Koala. And at this time, all the birds and animals lived forever, no one ever died. None of the creatures knew about death because they had never seen it.

Then one morning, a young Cockatoo was playing, high up in a tree. He called to the other animals,

> 'Corock, corock, look at me, swinging on a branch!'

The others looked up. He was very high. They watched him dance from branch to branch. Then, suddenly, he slipped and fell. All the way to the ground! With a loud 'whoomph' he landed on his head.

The other animals rushed up and saw the Cockatoo lying very still.

'What a good trick, Cockatoo!'

'Will you show us?'

'Didn't he look funny when he landed!'

But the Cockatoo didn't move. Perhaps he was embarrassed and hiding his face in the sand. Or perhaps he was just having a sleep. They tried to wake him, but they couldn't. He just lay there.

Then the wise old Wombat waddled up. He looked at the little Cockatoo lying there, his head to one side. The Wombat took a good look at the Cockatoo. Then he felt his tiny body, and turned to the other animals, telling them that the Cockatoo had broken his neck.

'What does that mean, Wombat?'

'Yes, Wombat, what does that mean?'

'Did the Spirits do it?'

The old Wombat thought for a while. The Spirits must have done this. They must have done this for a reason. But what reason? The Wombat called a meeting under a big old gum tree in the sandy creek bed.

All the animals came. The Snakes, the Crows, the Possums, the Emus, the Caterpillars, the Kangaroos — all the birds and animals.

'Tell us about the Cockatoo.'

'Sssshh! Did you see him fall, Wombat?'

'Is he still there?'

While they were talking, the Spirits came and took the little Cookatoo up into the sky. As the animals looked up, they could see the little Cockatoo wafting away into the sky. When the animals saw this, they were even more puzzled. What had happened to the Cockatoo, and what were the Spirits going to do with him? This had certainly never happened before.

Then the Wombat spoke, very slowly.

'I think, I think that the Spirits have taken the Cockatoo up into the sky, so they can change him into something else.'

The animals were confused, but they were also curious.

Then the Possum said,

'What if someone went up into the sky, and waited to see what the Spirits do with the little Cockatoo?'

The Wombat thought that this was an excellent idea. But who was to go? Wombat was certainly too old to be climbing around the sky. Anyway, it was nearly winter, and he had his burrow to fix. He asked the Snakes,

'Sssss, not usss, not usss — we're too sssleepy.'

So he asked the Crows,

> 'Coark, coark, well we'd like to, but . . .'

So he asked the Kangaroos,

> 'Don't send us, what about the Magpie Geese, they're always poking their noses into our business!'

So he asked the Magpie Geese,

> 'You only asked us because the Kangaroos said to!'

The Wombat was stuck. None of the animals wanted to go. He understood. It did mean spending the whole winter there; it would be cold, and there would be no shelter. Ah well, he thought, we'll never find out.

Then the Caterpillars wriggled up.

> 'What about us? We never get asked to do things. All of us could go together, then we can make our camp and spend the whole winter there. When it gets warm in the spring, we will come back and tell you what has happened to the little Cockatoo!'

The animals cheered. Good old Caterpillars! They would find out what happened to the little Cockatoo, even if it did mean spending the whole winter there.

So the Caterpillars gathered, and in one huge wriggling cloud, went up into the sky. And all the other animals sat down to wait for the spring.

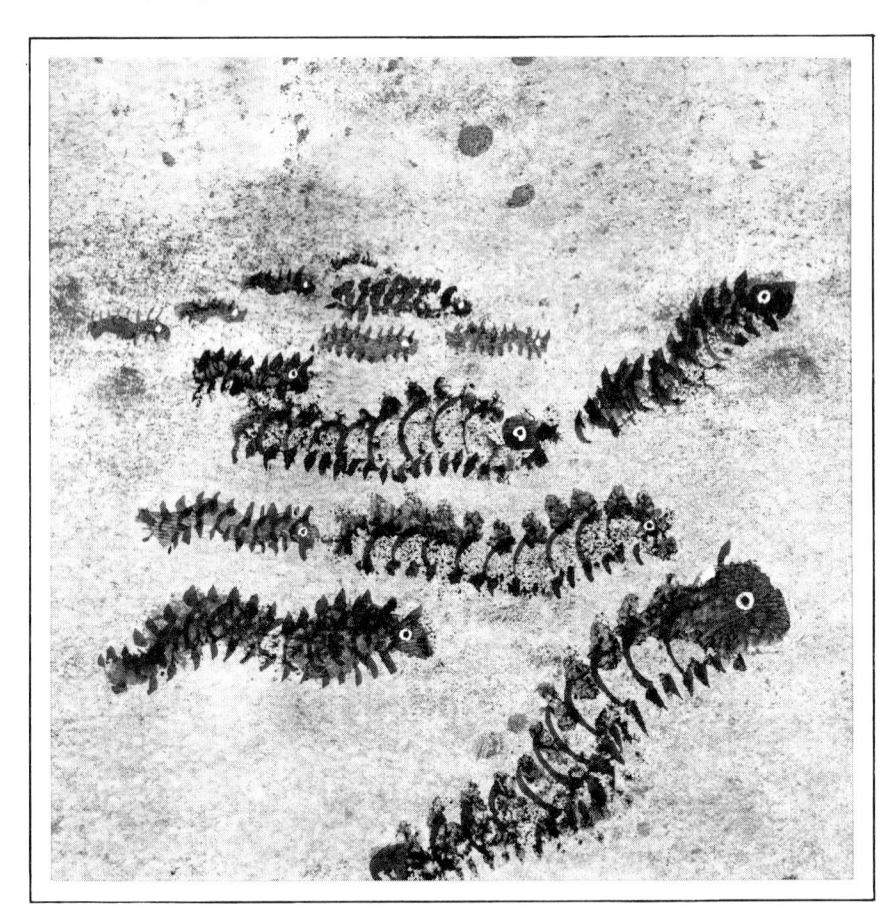

When the winter was nearly over, the Wombat called all the animals together. They agreed to send out a hunting party to look for the Caterpillars. The Snakes said they would go. But they found nothing.

The next day, the Crows flew off to look, but no Caterpillars. Each day, a group of animals would go out, searching for the Caterpillars, and each day they would return with nothing.

Then, on the first warm day of spring, a pair of Dragonflies came rushing back to where the animals were camped. They were very very excited,

> 'We have seen them! We have seen them! And they are different! They are returning with new bodies!'

Then the Dragonflies flew off to bring the Caterpillars back to where the animals were camped. The animals waited. What would the Caterpillars look like?

Then they saw them. A beautiful parade of brightly coloured wings! Reds and blues, whites and yellows. The first Butterflies!

As the Butterflies flicked and flitted, the animals realized that here was the proof that the Spirits had given the Caterpillars a new and beautiful shape.

They also realized that when the Spirits took the little Cockatoo, they took him so that they could give him a new shape, so that he could become a new creature.

As the Butterflies settled in the trees, they made such a pretty sight that the old ones decided that this must always be so.

So, ever since then, the caterpillars spend winter hidden in cocoons, preparing for the change into their beautiful spring bodies, just as they did long ago in the Dreamtime.

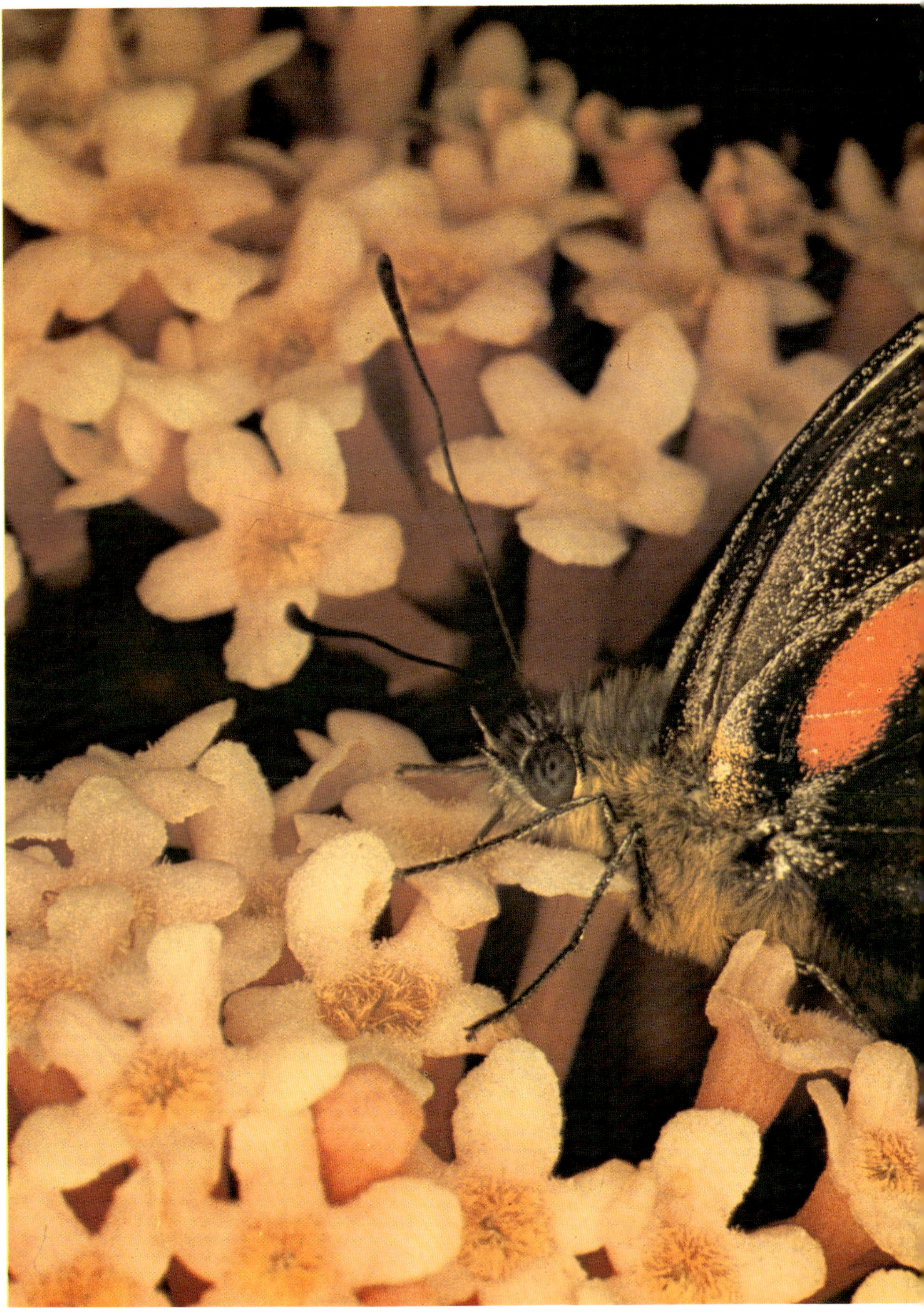